DITTON: THE STORY OF A K̶̶̶̶̶ISH VILLAGE

The stream at Church Mill with the tannery building on the left. This is a companion drawing to page 23, also drawn by J.C. Nattes on July 31st 1816.

Front cover: St Peter's Church and Ditton Court farmhouse from Bradbourne Lane in 1960, looking across field D of the rear cover

Back cover: John Hart's map of Ditton Court Farm drawn in 1772

Young fishermen at the Ditton Stream ford, circa 1953. Stream Cottage in the background

DITTON

The Story of a Kentish Village

To Gary & Coral
best wishes

Alan Dodge

Alan Dodge

September 2011

DITTON HERITAGE CENTRE

Published in 2011 by
Ditton Heritage Centre Ltd.
New Road
Ditton
Aylesford
Kent
ME20 6AE

Origination by Ex Libris Press
Bradford on Avon
www.ex-librisbooks.co.uk

Typeset in 11/16 point Palatino

Printed in Britain by
CPI Antony Rowe, Chippenham, Wiltshire

ISBN 978-0-9569567-0-5

The author was born in Bradbourne Lane, Ditton, in 1938. After attending the village school and Maidstone Grammar School he studied Biology at the University of London. He continued postgraduate research for a PhD in Plant Biochemistry and, until retirement, was a Senior Lecturer at the University of Bath. He is the author of *Freshford: The History of a Somerset Village*, where he has lived for over 45 years, and where he was a founder member and chairman of the Local History Society. He is organist of the village church and has been chairman of the Parish Council and a churchwarden. He is married to Margaret and has two sons and two daughters.

CONTENTS

	Acknowledgements and Thanks	6
	Introduction	7
Chapter 1	Setting the Scene	9
Chapter 2	Prehistoric and Roman History	24
Chapter 3	A Saxon and Norman Community	30
Chapter 4	Medieval Times: Church and Monastic Influence	39
Chapter 5	The Reformation to the Restoration	52
Chapter 6	A Georgian Village	64
Chapter 7	A Victorian Village	94
Chapter 8	War and Peace	122
Chapter 9	The Modern World	155
	Further Reading and References	170
	Index	173

ACKNOWLEDGEMENTS and THANKS

I should like to give especial thanks to Liz and John Day (the secretary and chairman of the Ditton Heritage Centre), to Tony and Maralyn Mulcuck, and to the other members of the Trust for their enthusiasm in supporting my idea of writing a book on the history of Ditton. Liz Day was a most helpful contact in Ditton for me from my home in Somerset, and efficiently enlisted financial support for the publication of this book. We are most grateful to the following for their generosity.

> Ditton Parish Council.
> Kent County Council.
> The Allen Grove Local History Fund of the Kent Archaeological Society.
> David Stevens.
> Theo Papa Adams of Papa's Fish and Chip Restaurant, Ditton.
> Kia Garage Ditton.

In Ditton I would also like to thank Simon Webley for his encouragement and hospitality, and to Ditton Parish Council and their Clerk, Sue Kavanagh, for access to the Parish Council Minutes and other records. To the East Malling Trust for Horticultural Research and to Lorraine Farman for access to Bradbourne House, and to Penny Greaves for expert photography in making a copy of the Ditton Court map of 1775 and for making other pictures available. To the staff of the Centre for Kentish Studies in Maidstone for their helpfulness and courtesy, and to the Kent Archaeological Society for the use of their excellent library in Maidstone Museum, and for permission to copy a figure from Archaeologia Cantiana. At the Museum, to Fiona Woolley for providing copies of drawings of Church Mill by Nattes. To the staff of the National Monuments Record at Swindon, the British Library, the Public Record Office, and the Incorporated Church Building Society for access to records. To my brother, Prof. John Dodge, for providing census information and the loan of books, and my son Dr. Christopher Dodge for expert assistance when my computer skills failed! It has been a pleasure to work again with Roger Jones of Ex Libris Press at Bradford on Avon, who has been responsible for the layout and design of this book. Finally, thanks to my wife Margaret for her expert editorial assistance and encouragement.

Grateful thanks to the following for illustrations. (page numbers, u=upper; m=middle; l=lower)

Centre for Kentish Studies, 49u, 70, 71, 77, 90, 91, 111, 124
Ditton Heritage Centre, 119
John Dodge, 88, 131, 159, and for the late William Dodge, 46, 136 150
East Malling Trust for Horticultural Research, 68, 80, 82, 83, 138, 141, 145, 152 l, 166, rear cover.
Kent Archaeological Society, 25
Kent Messenger, 3, 157u
Maidstone Museum and Art Gallery, 1, 23
National Monuments Record, Swindon, 49m, 105, 125, 145u
Joyce Parsons (née Scott), 99
Simon Webley, 67

The following are from the author's collection; Front Cover, 5, 11, 12, 14, 16, 18, 19, 20, 21, 26, 27, 32, 35, 27u, 37l, 38, 40, 42u, 42 l, 44 a and b, 48, 49 l, 50, 51, 53, 55, 56, 57, 59, 63, 72, 74, 76, 79, 81, 84, 85, 86, 92, 95, 101, 102, 103, 104, 106, 108, 109, 110u, 110 l, 112, 114u, 114 l, 115, 116, 117, 121, 123, 126, 127, 128u, 128 l, 129u, 129 l, 130, 132, 133, 135u, 135 l, 140, 142, 144, 147, 149, 151, 152u, 153, 154, 156, 157, 160, 161, 164, 165, 167, 168.

INTRODUCTION

'The history of an English parish is, in microcosm, the history of England'; so wrote the historian Sir Arthur Bryant in 1949. I have long contemplated writing the history of the microcosm of Ditton, and this has now proved possible with the enthusiastic support of the Ditton Heritage Centre. This Centre is located in the room where I started school in 1943!

I have long family associations with Ditton going back to 1879 when my great grandparents, John and Jane Dodge, moved from Hunton to Cobdown Farm Cottages. My grandfather also John (1868-1957) was 11 years old and, like his father, went to work on Cobdown Farm. In the census of 1881 he is described at the age of 12 as 'agricultural labourer'. He explained to me what Ditton was like before the rapid expansion in building of the mid 1880s when the whole of the area between Bell Lane and Orchard Grove was a large hop garden. He was too old for compulsory education himself but his younger siblings attended Ditton School, as did his own six children later after his marriage to Sarah. They lived in Daisy Bank in New Road, and my parents in Bradbourne Lane from 1932-1998.

My father told me much about the village before the First World War. It is hard to believe that less than 100 years ago he was sent to collect flour for family bread making from Mill Hall Mill. His work in local government enabled him to have access to large scale maps of the parish which marked such details as BS for boundary stone. It was a delight to rediscover a parish boundary stone at Ditton Common that he showed me over 60 years ago. I also have memories of Philip Scott, the rector, from 1943-55 showing me the enormous tithe map of 1841, and the late 17th century registers and churchwardens' account books, then located in the church chest.

I have been recording information about the history of Ditton since 1955, when I wrote about the history and natural history of the stream for a Sixth Form school project. At that time Allen Grove, the Curator of Maidstone Museum, gave me advice and encouragement, and pointed me to the helpful archivists in the Kent Archives Office.

These influences of aural recollection, physical artefacts and boundaries, as well as a wealth of unpublished information from maps and manuscripts, are the basis of the local historian's sources. I have used all of these as well as published works and pictures to produce this chronological history of the 'microcosm' of Ditton. I dedicate it to the memory of my parents, William and Olive.

Alan Dodge, 2011

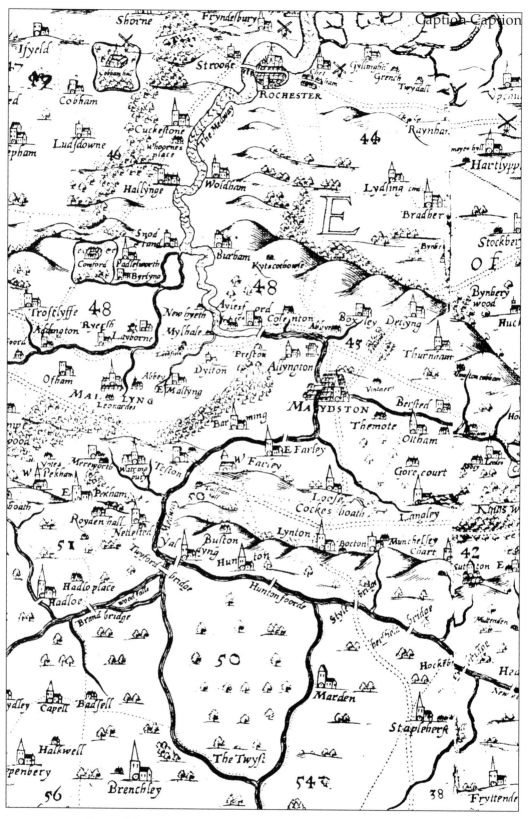

Part of the map of Kent drawn by Philip Symonson in 1596.
This is the first map of Kent to show roads.

Chapter 1

Setting the Scene

'This parish is rather an obscure place.'

History and Topographical Survey of the County of Kent
Edward Hasted, 1732-1812

Introduction

When Edward Hasted wrote these words about Ditton in 1798, it was by contrast to its larger and more influential neighbouring parishes of Aylesford and East Malling, easily overlooked. Over the centuries it has been a place quickly passed through either on the river Medway, turnpike, railway, and now Motorway, without much comment. Hasted wrote:

The high road from London, through Wrotham, to Maidstone, crosses the middle of it, at the thirty-first milestone; the village stands on it, and the church about a quarter of a mile further southward, on an ascent, beyond which, the parish reaches into the large tract of coppice woods. The stream, from Bradbourne park runs through the parish and village, across the above road, and having turned two mills, runs on to the river Medway.

This stream, still an important and conspicuous feature of the village, was certainly the key reason for a small settlement here, simply described by Hasted as: called in ancient records *Dictune*. It takes its name from the Saxon words *dic* and *tune*, which signify the village situated on the dike, or trench of water. The Saxon/Old English *dic* became quite widely used in the number of Ditton place names throughout England in Cambridge, Cheshire, Shropshire and Surrey, as well as villages such as Ditcheat and Ditchling. The Old English *tun* variously describing an enclosure, farmstead, village manor or estate, is one of the most widely used English place name elements as also shown in the local villages of Allington, Addington, Cuxton, Hunton and Linton.

Ditton remained a small agriculturally based community from Domesday times (1086) until the early 1800s with relatively little population change apart from during the Black Death. However, there has been considerable development within the last two hundred years, the population increasing from 98 in 1801 to 4,753 in 2001, nearly a fifty-fold increase. In the same period Aylesford increased five fold and East Malling eleven-fold. There has been extensive house building, industrial development, quarrying, road building, and also the unfortunate demolition of so many significant historic buildings, such as Borough Court and farm, Ditton Court and farm, Ditton Place and farm, Mill Hall Mill, Fernleigh House, Ivy House, Lone Barn and The Rectory (in Kiln Barn Road). Thus, with this overlaying of development and the loss of buildings, field patterns, and woodland, it is much harder to perceive what David Cecil (1948) wrote of Thomas Gray:

> To him no place existed only in the present. Behind the England of his own day, he discerned as in a vision the long perspective of the past, peopled with figures of bygone generations, stretching away to the dim horizons of antiquity.

Nevertheless, the vanished places and old cottage sites marked on early maps, together with the few old buildings that remain, such as Cobdown Farm, Church Mill (The Old Millhouse), Stream Cottages and above all St Peter's Church, still remind us that on this land our forefathers lived, and laboured in the fields, woods, mills, and worshipped in the church for a thousand or more years.

The Parish in View

Ditton is located on the gentle northern slope of the east-west greensand ridge, often called the Chart Hills (*Chart* means a rough common), that crosses the northern weald of Kent. From a southerly high border with the parish of Barming at about 300 feet above sea level, it drops northward to the tidal reaches of the river Medway three miles away. At no point is the parish more than three quarters of a mile wide. From the southern border the upper reach of the river Medway, now not tidal, is only three quarters of a mile away, the river having cut a wide arc through the Chart hills at Maidstone. The long western boundary of the parish is with East Malling including Larkfield and New Hythe, and the eastern boundary is with the parish of Aylesford. The area of Ditton at the beginning of the 20th century was 1,073 acres in contrast to the much larger adjacent villages of East Malling with 2,789 acres and Aylesford 4,377. From Saxon times it was in the lathe (a sub division of the Kingdom of Kent) of Aylesford which was a major part of mid-west Kent, and in lathe subdivision, the Hundred of Larkfield. Hundreds originally consisted of 100 hides of land, (a hide was between 60-100 acres) and the Hundred Courts met, probably in the open air and later in a court house, at nearby Larkfield, to transact business and solve Hundred disputes. The area of the hundred consisted of Ditton, Aylesford, Wouldham, Burham, Allington, Snodland (with Padlesworth) Birling, Ryarsh, Leybourne, East and West Malling, Offham, Addington and Trottiscliffe. This Hundred grouping of parishes formed the basis for the Malling Poor Law Union of the 1830s and then of Malling Rural District in the 1890s. Although located only three to four miles west of Maidstone, local government and parliamentary representation has always extended to links with Sevenoaks or Tonbridge. Likewise the ecclesiastical links are with the Diocese of Rochester, founded in 604, rather than with Maidstone in the Diocese of Canterbury.

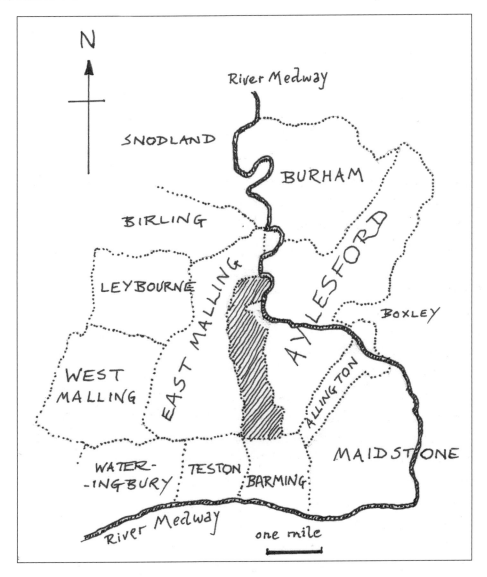

Ditton, shaded, and neighbouring parishes

The boundaries of the parish of Ditton today are probably very similar to those established in the 11th or 12th century. The evolution of a parish from Norman manors/estates followed the independence of the manor church/chapel from the Minster church and the need to provide support for its priest from the tithes (tenth of crops) from a defined area. Thus the parish of Ditton was defined following in the north the natural boundary of the river Medway, and then in other parts by field boundaries or other geographical features, including an ancient earthwork at **Well Wood**. The parish was allocated a range of land types (a very common feature of down/valley parishes) embracing from the north, riverside meadows and pasture, then well drained and productive arable land, and woodland on the higher, more stony ground. In this way the parish, with its stream to provide water and power, could be reasonably self-sufficient in food and fuel. In course of time this ecclesiastical parish became the basis of a local government unit, governed by the Vestry with responsibilities for the poor and needy, roads and public order. Thus boundary markers were reinforced as being the limit of parochial responsibility, by identification with pollarded tree stumps and boundary stones, some of which are clearly marked on 19th century Ordnance Survey maps, and may even be found today, such as a stone at Ditton Common on the border with Barming.

A boundary stone at Ditton Common on the Ditton/Barming border

Places and Names

Through much of its recorded history Ditton possessed two manors, Ditton Court and Borough Court. *Court* is a term widely used in place of *Manor* in Kent, and indicates the former centres of manorial government. From Norman times the manorial court would meet to consider matters such as land tenure and the organisation of communal agriculture, services owed by tenants to the lord of the manor, and issues of petty crime. In England, parish churches were often built at the instigation of the Lord of the manor adjacent to his residence. **Ditton Court** was no exception and until demolition in 1972 to make way for Ditton Court Close, it was a few yards to the west of St Peter's Church. Over the centuries the powers of the manor diminished, many being taken over by local government, but the name is a reminder of feudal England. **Borough Court**, also known as Brooke Court, and variously spelt in record as Burrough or Brook, was in the northern part of the parish near New Hythe and the river Medway. The name *Borough* often indicates that a manor crosses two parishes, here Ditton and East Malling. The court of this manor still met into the second half of the 19th century, at the Bull Inn in Larkfield. The alternative name for this manor, *Brooke* is probably derived from the Kentish term *brook* that was used for water meadows, which would be most appropriate for this situation near the River Medway. Borough Court and farm were demolished during the expansion of Reed's paper mills in the 1920s. In addition to these manors and their estates, the other major historical land units in the parish have been associated with Ditton Place and Cobdown Farm. **Ditton Place** was referred to by Hasted in 1798 as a 'mansion in this parish'. The designation *Place* means a country house with grounds, and was also used locally for houses in West Malling, Addington and Birling. The farm associated with Ditton Place was demolished during road widening of the A20 in 1927. Ditton Place itself was demolished after a fire in 1987 and is now the site of Troutbeck House. Cobdown Farm was the name given to the long established Ditton Farm after the building of Cobdown House in 1856. The name **Cobdown** was taken from the nearby hill called Copdowne in 1684 and Coptdown in 1842, possibly having a link to a copped or coppiced tree or trees on this small hill.

In the south of the parish is the area of **Kiln Barn** which originated as a small farm settlement at a spring in the early 19th century. Later it was part of Ditton Court Farm and the site of some hop-pickers' huts. The name is derived from the presence in the area of a lime kiln. A large field to the north of the settlement and dissected by the railway in 1874 was called Kiln Field, after the existence of a double limekiln. The kiln was used for heating chalk, obtained from the North Downs, to give the more useful lime (calcium oxide) utilised in the village tanneries as well as in agriculture and in building. There would have been a good supply of coppice wood fuel nearby from Spickets Wood, Knoxes Shaw, Palmer's Rough, Coal Pits Wood, as well as the extensive Oaken Wood.

For hundreds of years Ditton had two water powered corn grinding mills. One was located next to the Old Mill House at The Stream, and due to its proximity to the church was usually referred to as **Church Mill**. The other, **Mill Hall Mill,**

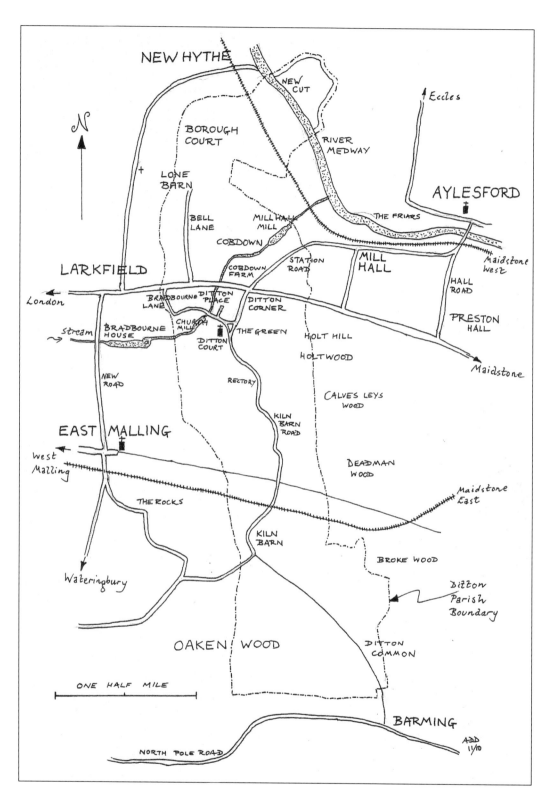

The major historical features of Ditton and area

took its name from the nearby Medway wharf hamlet in Aylesford of Mill Hall. As there is no other possible mill site at Mill Hall, the linked name could be derived from an association between this mill and a manorial 'hall' (see chapter 3). The old mill house and most of the mill building was demolished by Reeds in 1946, but the mill wheel remained until the construction of the M20. The name Mill Hall distinguishes this area from the nearby house and ancient estate of **Preston Hall,** so called for its association with an endowment to support a priest (*priest-ton*). Another name used for Mill Hall Mill in the late 18th and early 19th centuries was **Coldharbour.** This is a name usually associated with a place where animals (cattle and sheep) could be held overnight or during inclement conditions. It is likely that the London Road was an important drove way, and the cold harbour, here as well another towards Allington, were useful stopping places for drovers.

At the time of the Tithe award survey of Ditton in 1841 approximately one third of the parish was woodland of which over 200 acres were in **Oaken Wood.** The name probably goes back to Saxon times when the word ending –*en* was used in Southern England to signify the plural as in *ox* and *oxen*. On Symonson's 1596 map of Kent, this wood stretched along the Chart Hill ridge from Teston and East Malling almost as far as Allington, making a wooded barrier between Ditton and Maidstone. The oak was a most important source of timber in Kent for ship and house building. Oak standard trees are present in the woods today, interspersed among extensive chestnut coppice. On present day maps the southern part of Oaken Wood is still called **Ditton Common.** Common land, available to all village dwellers, was an important feature of medieval and post medieval livelihood. There was often an opportunity for the grazing of animals and fowls, and the availability of brushwood and timber. Squatters sometimes erected primitive residences on it. The 22 acres of the Common were sold and enclosed in 1859 in exchange for small payments to village landowners and the provision of allotments for the others. The other major area of woodland in the 1841 survey was **Holt Wood** which occupied a delightful hilly position between Ditton and Aylesford. *Holt* is an Old English name for a wood or wooded hill, but now the houses of Woodlands Road, Acorn Drive, Cedar Close and Birch Crescent, have mostly replaced the trees. Other woods of some size in the 18th century, included a 24 acre **Palmars Rough** (var. Palmers Rough/Ruff) to the east of Kiln Barn Road, and a 12 acre **Coal Pits** at Kiln Barn. This surprising name signifies that this wood was used for charcoal production. Charcoal burning pits have been identified in Saxon England, and this pit technique was superseded by earth covered stacks in the 16th century. A small wood at Kiln Barn called **Spickets Wood** is called **Pickets Wood** on a map of 1772. The word *pike* was sometimes used to describe a triangular field, and this might have been the shape of this wood before much clearance. A nearby wood is called **Knoxes Shaw/ Wood** where a *shaw* is name for a copse or small wood. The origin of *Knox* could be the same as for *Knockholt = oak wood*. The Anglo Saxon word for oak, *oc* to which the *n* is derived from words meaning 'at the'. **Broke Wood** on the border with Aylesford, and now decimated by quarrying, might owe its name to the presence of badgers. The Saxon name for this animal was *brocc*.

Chestnut coppice in Oaken Wood in 1961. Now destroyed by quarrying

The ancient road pattern of Ditton consists of a major east-west road crossing the parish and leading from London to the east, and a few branches to the north and south. Through history this has been variously called **The Maidstone Road** or **The London Road** and was turnpiked in 1773. After the A2, Watling Street, in north Kent, it was the second most important road between London and the channel ports, hence its 20th century designation A20. Arising from this, the direct road to Aylesford from Ditton Corner was called **Station Road** after the opening of Aylesford Station on the Strood to Maidstone railway line in 1856. Previously this road was known as Mill Hall Road, or in 1684 the 'Road to Mill Hale'. The other old road on the north side is **Bell Lane**. This was predominantly a farm road/track leading to Borough Court Farm and to fields in the north of the village and the river Medway. Prior to major building on the east side of Bell Lane in the 1880s a large field between the lane and what is now Orchard Grove was called Bell Field/Ground. Fields with the name Bell in other parts of England have been associated with the provision of income for new church bell ropes, but there is no evidence of this association here. Until the construction of New Road in 1870 linking the Green with Ditton Corner, the main southerly route from the London Road to the church and village green was **Ditton Street.** This ran from opposite Cobdown Farm skirting the rear of Ditton Place, but was closed for much of its length in 1860 on the construction of a **New Road.** *New* is a relative term, as this is also the name for the road from Larkfield to East Malling made new after a diversion in 1676, and New Hythe, a new landing place hundreds of years old on the river Medway! From The Green, Kiln Barn Road proceeds in the direction of Kiln Barn, Ditton Common, and East Malling and from the nearby stream, **Bradbourne Lane** passes through the unique lengthy stream ford and on to the rear of the Bradbourne estate and the London Road. The stream had previously passed through the park of Bradbourne House from which it got its name in Tudor times. *Brad burna* is Anglo Saxon for broad stream.

Over the years many paths and rights of way have been diverted or lost. One lane that has vanished completely was called **Old Ead Lane** in 1775. It ran from the direction of Borough Court to the river Medway, and was also a direct access via Bell Lane for the village as a whole to the river. Where the lane joined the river's edge a field was called *Old Hide (Hythe) Field* in 1681 and *Old Hithe Field* in 1841. This was possibly an important wharf site before the development of the *New Hythe* half a mile down river. *Ead* might have been a corruption of the Old English word for a river, *Ea,* as found in place names like Eaton.

Field patterns and field names are an important feature of village history. The most complete reference to these is the Tithe Survey of the whole parish in 1841. A comparison of this record with earlier farm surveys of Borough Court in 1681 and 1750, Ditton Farm (Cobdown) in 1684 and Ditton Court in 1772 shows some changes in field pattern, farm roads and names. As with most parishes the names followed various themes such as field size: *Two, Four, Five, Seven and Eight acres;* shape: *Shoulder of Mutton, Long, Great;* crop grown *Hop Ground, Orchard, Paddoc;,* other features, not always identifiable: *Kiln, Bell, Crowplain, Crabtree, Bagwood, Papermill, Chequer, Budland;* other plants: *Banky Broom, Rushy and Ozier;* uncertain, crossing the Aylesford border: *Upper* and *Lower nameless!*

Geology and Landscape

The Lower Greensand ridge on which most of Ditton is located originated as marine sediment 80-120 million years ago. Three of the four components of the Greensand are found within the parish and are classified as Hythe Beds, Sandgate Beds and Folkestone Beds. The lowest, Hythe Beds, consists of bands of limestone, known as Kentish rag, with interspersed sandy layers known as hassock. It is nearest to the surface from The Green southwards to Ditton Common. Major

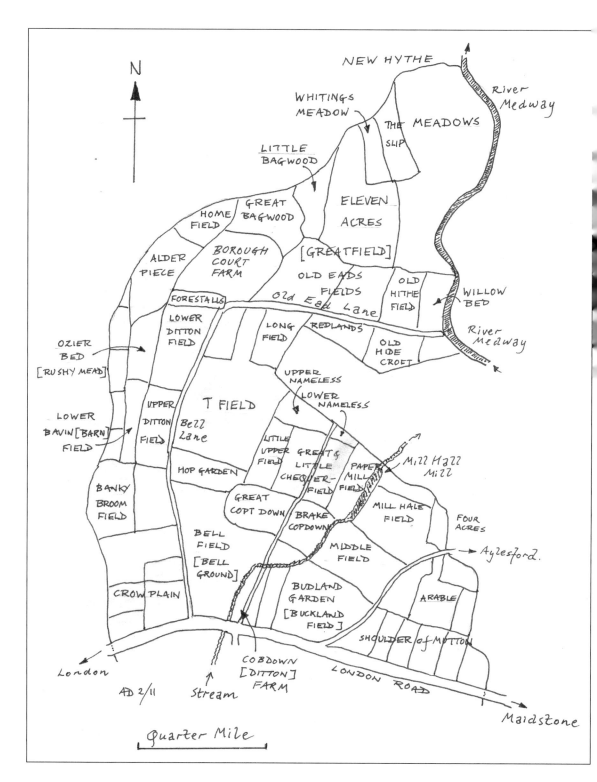

Field names in the north of the parish, based on maps of 1681, 1741 and 1841

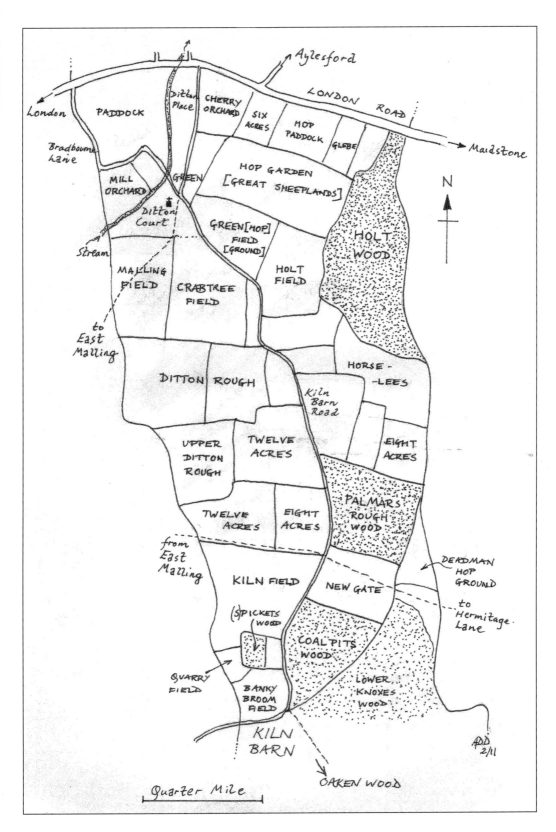

Field names in the south of the parish, based on maps of 1772 and 1841

quarries for the extraction of stone were established at Kiln Barn in the late 19th century, and nearer to the village in 1932 and more recently near Oaken Wood. Most of the stone from these quarries was tar-macadamised for road surfacing. Smaller old quarries were located on the Green and in Stream Lane. St Peter's Church is built predominantly of local ragstone and on the natural foundation of ragstone, to the displeasure of generations of grave diggers! This stone was not used to any major extent in other village buildings until after 1850. The building

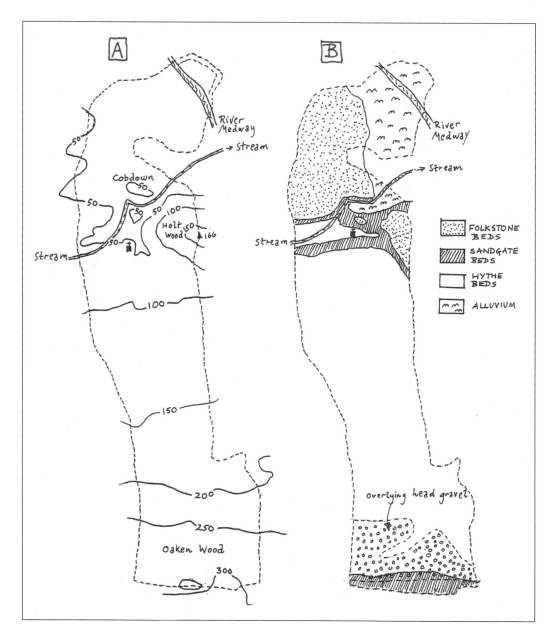

Physical features
A. *Height in feet above sea level*
B. *Geological strata*

of the new Preston Hall, completed in 1857 of locally quarried ragstone rather than brick, was followed by the erection on the estate of numerous stone cottages, school buildings and farms, including Ditton School and Ditton Court Farm. Over millennia the Hythe Beds weathered to give good soil, some classified by soil scientists as Ditton Series, and excellent for fruit growing. It is not surprising that the first fields obtained for Wye College's experimental fruit research station in 1913 were part of Ditton Court Farm. This subsequently became East Malling Research Station. Overlaying the Hythe Beds in an area to the north west of the stream, including Cobdown and the outlier of Holt Hill, are the two sandy layers of Sandgate and Folkestone Beds. Sandpits existed at the London Road end of Bradbourne Lane and just across the parish boundary near New Hythe Church. These areas with more acid soil were particularly good for pine trees and other conifers and there was much planting of such trees during the mid-19th century in the landscaped parks around Cobdown House, Ditton Place and Preston Hall, and in the gardens of Fernleigh and the former Rectory. Both Cobdown and Preston Hall (in Holt Wood) had summerhouses on hilltops landscaped with conifers. In spite of much tree felling and subsequent development, vestiges of these plantings can still be seen after 150 years.

South-west corner of the nave of St Peter's Church. The light coloured quoins are of tufa, a limestone deposited in the stream valley. The darkest stone is carstone, an iron containing sandstone from the Folkestone Beds. The remainder is mostly ragstone from the Hythe Beds

To the north of Cobdown and towards the river Medway, alluvial soil made for good pasture and arable land, as at Borough Court Farm. There was less fruit and hop growing here in contrast to the other village farms. At the other end of the parish in Oaken Wood and Ditton Common, the Hythe Beds were overlaid with head gravel, making cultivation for crops difficult, but was satisfactory for the growth of woodland trees. There has probably been continuous management of woodland in this area from well before Domesday in 1086 when there was 'pannage for six pigs,' to 1798 when it was described as 'the large tract of coppice woods' (Hasted, 1798). The woods provided timber for house construction, fuel, charcoal, and oak bark for the village tanneries.

Apart from the largely Norman (11th-12th century) stone church, the oldest buildings remaining in Ditton are of timber construction: The Old Stream Cottage from about 1450, and the slightly later Old Mill House. Just over the border in Larkfield is the remarkable early timber house, The Wealden Hall which was erected in about 1350. Bricks made their appearance in the 16th century, and Borough Court was believed to have been built or rebuilt at this time. Cobdown Farmhouse (Ditton Farm) was built of red bricks in the 17th century, with bricks possibly made locally at brickfields at East Malling Heath, or West Malling. This farm together with Borough Court and Mill Hall Mill were part of the Twisden family's Bradbourne estates from the mid 17th century. Their rebuilding of Bradbourne House in the early 18th century is claimed to be one of the finest examples of domestic brickwork in the whole of England. Local red bricks were used for the four early 19th century cottages in Stream Lane, and a few decades later for the oast houses and cottages of Cobdown Farm, and the cottages in Pleasant Row in Station Road. Extensive brickworks were established in Burham and Aylesford in the mid 19th century which produced yellow bricks from clays containing less iron. These bricks were widely used in the locality for the building of new terraces in New Road, London Road and Bell Lane. Subsequent house building in the 20th and 21st centuries has used materials and styles without any particularly local influence or resource, giving here, as in almost all English speculatively built estates a dull uniformity. These are not of local style and materials, and are easily identified as of '30s, '60s, '90s and '00s! A notable exception were houses built on the Aylesford/Ditton border at Holt Wood in the 1930s which used vernacular styles of building and materials, as well as a generous spatial layout, and maintaining as many trees as possible.

Water, in the stream flowing from East Malling, was the fundamental factor for the placing of the settlement that was eventually to become Ditton. The Hythe Beds of the Lower Greensand act as an efficient aquifer, and as with the chalk hills, springs will break out at the juxtaposition of the Hythe Beds with a lower impermeable layer. In this locality there are important springs on the north

Church Mill, Ditton. A drawing by J.C. Nattes on July 31st, 1816

side of the Chart Hills at West and East Malling. Those at East Malling are at Springhead, linked to the appropriately named Broadwater, and also at Gillet's Hollow, nearer the village centre. In the stream valleys, calcium deposits gave rise to tufa, a stone that could more easily be cut into quoins, which are found in the walls of both Ditton and East Malling churches. These two streams from East Malling merge at Bradbourne and flow through Ditton as one stream. Over the centuries this stream has provided in these two parishes drinking water for humans and animals, power for six mills, (three corn and three paper), ornamental features for parks and gardens, water for tanneries, and enjoyment for children! This is the chronological story of a community on a stream, *Dictune*/Ditton.

Chapter 2

Prehistoric and Roman History to AD 410

Britain is rich in grain and timber, it has good pasturage for cattle and draft animals and it is well known for its plentiful springs and rivers.

Ecclesiastical History of the English People: Bede, 673-735

The first evidence of the existence of man in this immediate area is from the Middle Stone Age, also known as the Mesolithic period 7,000-8,000 BC. In the 1930s a collection of flint tools from this time were found in East Malling (Clark, 1932) and in 1964 during building work at Holt Wood, 58 flints were discovered (Palmer, 1965). About fifteen of the flints were implements such as scrapers and blades. Flints were easily available from the North Downs for tool manufacture by nomadic hunters who could have travelled from what we now call the European mainland. It is thought that these meolithic travellers might have used the route of the Medway valley. This was at a time when 'England' was still joined to the continent. The separation took place in about 5,000 BC. A large collection of tools of this period was found at Oldbury Hill in Ightham. From about 10,000 BC trees and shrubs such as birch and pine, and later hazel, oak, alder, elm and ash would have gradually covered this area, and the hunters would be seeking animals such as deer, reindeer and horses. They would be well provided with water from the streams and rivers. It was a few thousand years later in the New Stone Age (Neolithic) that the first settled farms were established circa 4000-3000BC. The earliest known site in England is at Windmill Hill near Avebury in Wiltshire. Here a notable long barrow (West Kennet) was constructed for burial. In the Medway Gap about three miles to the north-east of Ditton in Aylesford are the remains of two Neolithic long barrows, at Kits Coty and the Countless Stones. Three to four miles to the west are further burial sites at Addington and Coldrum in Trottiscliffe. As with the Wiltshire examples there are tomb gateways and a circle (at Coldrum) constructed of sarsen megaliths found on the nearby chalk hills. These are some of the most important archaeological remains in Kent, and show that in this area a pattern of settled farming with small cultivated plots and herds of cattle had begun about five thousand years ago, which continue to this day. Perhaps there was communication between these two sites across a ford at Aylesford, a very important river crossing from earliest times, and possibly linked by a track-way passing through Ditton. It is possible that other burial mounds existed in this area but may have been destroyed with time.

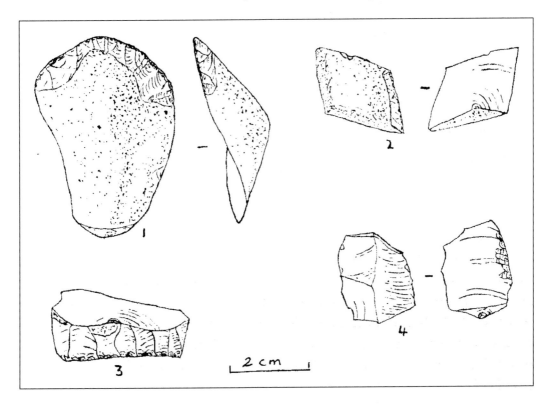

Flint artefacts from Holt Hill. Flint 1 is an end scraper; 2 is a side scraper; 3 is a scraper; 4 part of a small blade. From Palmer, 1965

The proximity of Kent to the rest of Europe has meant that it has always been in the front line for invasion. Settlers from the continent are more likely to have stayed in areas already cultivated in the Medway gap and to have ignored the densely wooded Weald and the slopes of the North Downs. From around 1800 BC arrivals from the continent brought distinctive pottery as well as copper for tools and weapons. This has given rise to the identification of these people as Beaker people, and the period of time from 1,800-550 BC as the Bronze Age. The imported copper was smelted with tin to produce the harder and more useful alloy, bronze. It is likely that in this area, already well settled from the Stone Age, there was a gradual clearing of woodland to give more land for crops. Farming became more efficient with the establishment of fields, an increase in sheep production for wool, and from about 900 BC the introduction of a plough. Burial of the dead was now in round barrows rather than the former long barrows. There is little evidence of their existence in this area, probably due to later ploughing. The importance of metal at this time is demonstrated by the discovery of bronze tools, ornaments, vessels and weapons, while gold was used for ornaments. The presence of 'important' people in this area is revealed by the finding of a collection of gold bracelets at Aylesford. From 550 BC to the arrival of the Romans in 55 BC, was the period known as the Iron Age from the arrival of this important hard metal for tools and weapons. Farmers now had the ability to store grain and keep cattle, sheep and pigs, and lived in circular huts, usually with a central hearth. Aylesford probably continued to be the centre of 'administration/power' judging from the nationally important burial findings discovered in 1886 and now in the British Museum (Evans, 1890). A number of chalk lined graves were identified in a sand pit, containing various cremation ash vessels, including one bucket-shaped decorated with a bronze frieze of horses, with a jug and pan imported from Italy. Such was the significance to archaeologists of this type of Iron Age burial that they were called *Aylesford-Swarling,* being some of the most important early finds of early Iron Age art.

Bronze Age pail (10 inches high) discovered at Aylesford in 1886. From Evans, 1890

One of the distinctive features of Iron Age civilisation was the establishment of hill forts. These defensive enclosures are particularly conspicuous in Wessex, for example at Maiden Castle in Dorset and Cadbury Castle in Somerset. The most important in this area, and indeed the largest in Kent, is at Oldbury Hill at Ightham. Here the hill top ditches enclose an area of over 50 hectares (123 acres) which still has conspicuous earthworks. To the east at Quarry Wood Camp near Loose there is evidence of another defensive earthwork. Small defensive or farm based earthworks have sometimes survived into the present age because the ground has been uncultivated as grassland or woodland. A small earthwork enclosure was identified by 19th century map makers on the boundary of Ditton and Aylesford between Well Wood and Broke Wood around half a mile east of Kiln Barn. This was rectangular in shape with dimensions of 100 by 50 metres (Page, 1908). Although described as 'An ancient Village Site', this could possibly have been a small late Bronze Age or Iron Age farming settlement. Such earthworks are known throughout England. They are more likely to be associated with animal enclosure than defence, and could have enclosed some huts as a small settlement. A well site has been identified in the south-west corner providing essential water in this area far from springs or streams. The lack of a good water supply could have been the reason for the demise of the settlement. The diversion

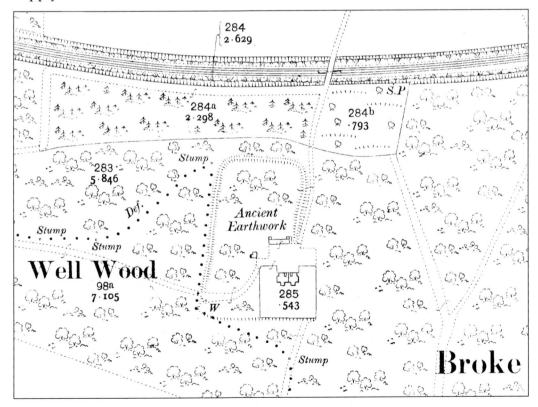

Map of Well Wood and Broke Wood showing the possible Bronze Age/Iron Age earthwork. From the 25 inch Ordnance Survey map of 1908.

of the Ditton - Aylesford parish boundary to include the western earthwork bank almost certainly indicates that this structure is of considerable antiquity, as is perhaps the name Well Wood. In the 19th century a pair of keepers' cottages (now demolished) were constructed within the enclosure as part of the Preston Hall estate.

In the hundred or so years before the first Roman invasion from recently conquered Gaul, trade and the interchange of goods between Britain and the continent had increased. This was facilitated by the use of coins of gold, silver or bronze. In the summers of 55 and 54 BC, Julius Caesar made two expeditions to Britain. Although both involved some skirmishes, some hostage taking and general reconnaissance, the onset of winter made him withdraw. Nearly one hundred years later in 43 AD another Roman invasion of around 40,000 men led by Aulus Plautius was dispatched from Gaul at the instigation of the Emperor Claudius. The major landing site was near present day Deal, but a better anchorage and defensive site was soon constructed at *Rutupiae* (Richborough) Kent (*Cantium*) at that time appears to have consisted of four different tribes, and there was relatively little resistance until the Roman army reached the River Medway. The course of the invading army through Kent is debatable. It could have followed a northerly route along what was to become Watling Street, or along the well defined route of the North Downs Way. One of the most important battles of the Roman conquest was thought to have taken place at the River Medway, although evidence for this site is equivocal. This battle took place over two days, and once the river was crossed, Plautius' army made for London. It is possible that the river crossing was between Aylesford and Rochester and if so, Britons living in this part of Kent would have been only too well aware of an enormous invasion force and some may well have been killed in battle. A military force of such strength was probably not seen in these parts until the reverse passage 1,900 years later in 1944 of an invasion force for the allied D-day landings in northern France.

With the arrival of the conquering Roman army, Cantium became part of the Roman Empire for nearly four hundred years. The most conspicuous features remaining of their presence and influence are the towns of Canterbury (*Durovernum*), Rochester (*Durobrivae*) and Dover (*Portus Dubris*), as well as the Roman roads of Watling Street and Stone Street and less obviously, the numerous villas that have been and continue to be discovered throughout the county. Although none have been found in Ditton, there are a number of sites within and around the Medway valley, including Maidstone, Barming, Teston, Snodland and Burham. Even nearer to Ditton is a villa site just to the north east of St James' Church at East Malling. The discovery of remnants of wall mosaics and wall plaster indicate that this was a building of some importance (Pirie, 1957;

Wacher, 1965). Although excavated in the 1960s, a late 19th century writer had previously claimed that material from Roman buildings had been incorporated into St. James' chancel walls (Fielding, 1893). About half a mile north of East Malling church and in the former park of Bradbourne House a Roman cemetery was discovered in 1996. This consisted of skeletons, evidences of cremation and some pottery. This confirmed a suggestion made by Fielding in 1893, that there was a Roman cemetery in Larkfield after the discovery of Roman urns. Another Roman cemetery was located at Holborough in Snodland which contained a magnificent lead coffin, now in Maidstone Museum.

Evidence from an important Iron Age burial (see above) suggests that Aylesford was the centre of local administration. The discovery of a large and luxurious Roman villa near Eccles, only half a mile from the River Medway north border of Ditton might confirm this. The villa was established in the early years of the Roman occupation on the site of an Iron Age farmstead. Eventually this villa had 12 rooms and a Bath House. It was the centre of a large farming enterprise coupled with pottery and tile manufacture, a trade that was to figure prominently in Aylesford's 19th century economy. A link between this area and other important centres of Roman population was provided by a road which ran from Rochester to Maidstone via Blue Bell Hill. Maidstone became an increasingly important town located on this Roman road which is evident today in the line of Week Street and Stone Street, and proceeding south to the iron producing area of the Weald. Located on the River Medway, Maidstone became a significant inland port for the transport of the locally quarried ragstone by boat to *Londinium* (London) for the building of defensive walls.

Roman influence had been gradually diminishing and finally came to an end in 410, which paved the way for Saxon invaders. In addition to a communication legacy, the Romans brought a number of important crops such as apples, cherries, grapes and mulberries. Their love of fruit led them to introduce orchards, and also, it is believed, both the sweet chestnut and walnut trees, and the technique of coppicing. Thus although no tangible Roman remains exist in Ditton, orchards and sweet chestnut coppice still figure as important features of the local economy as they have for hundreds of years.

Chapter 3

An Anglo Saxon and Norman Community, 410-1154

The Saxon is not like the Normans. His manners are not so polite.
But he never means anything serious till he talks about justice and right.

Norman and Saxon (A.D. 1100)   Rudyard Kipling, 1865-1936

Invaders from the continent after the end of Roman rule, according to Bede in 731, 'were from the three most formidable races of Germany; the Saxons, Angles and Jutes. From the Jutes are descended the people of Kent and the Isle of Wight' (Bede, 1980). A longstanding local tradition based on the uncertain evidence of Bede and the *Anglo Saxon Chronicle* is a link between two Jutish brothers Hengist and Horsa and Aylesford. In 449 a Kentish King Vortigern had invited them to assist in his battles with a reward of land in Kent. They came, but in 455 'fought against Vortigen the king in the place which is called Agelesford [Aylesford?], and his brother Horsa was killed. And after that Hengist succeeded to the kingdom.' (Swanton, 1997). It has been suggested that after Roman withdrawal there was a decline in population and any residual Christianity, clearly shown to be present as in the Roman villa at Lullingstone, declined or was replaced. Evidence of early Anglo Saxon settlements is limited, but provided by the existence of burial sites. One has been identified on Holborough Hill at Snodland, and the discovery of a Saxon spear at Cobdown in Ditton in 1962 could possibly indicate a burial site here. Burial with weapons was quite a common custom at that time (Kelly, 1962).

In 597 an event happened in Kent that was to change every town and village for good. Pope Gregory decided to send a Christian missionary, Augustine, to a land that he described as 'England placed in the corner of the world, (which) still remained without faith in the worship of stocks and stones' (Gee and Hardy, 1896). The acceptance of Augustine by King Ethelbert of Kent and by his French wife Bertha, and the establishment of a Christian church at Canterbury was the first step in the re-Christianisation of Kent. The foundation of the Diocese of Canterbury in 597, with Augustine as its first bishop, encompassed much land in the county to the east of the River Medway. In 604 the diocese and cathedral of Rochester were founded, and the diocese included land mostly to the west of the Medway, with Justus as the first bishop. From these small beginnings the next six hundred years saw the establishment and construction in Kent alone of about five hundred churches, including that of St Peter, Ditton, well before the Norman Conquest in 1066.

The major Roman estate at present day Eccles probably continued into the Saxon period, and then after the establishment of the Diocese of Rochester could have become an important religious centre. Eccles is derived from the British word for church, *egles* which is derived from the Greek word *ekklesia*. At the time of the Domesday survey in 1086 the large manor of Aylesford was a royal manor held by King William. This could have been the remaining centre of a large royal estate of many thousands of acres that dominated this part of Kent. The subsequent designation of the Lathe of Aylesford with its constituent Hundreds stretching across the whole of mid-west Kent would support this idea. Such an estate would have a minster church at its centre at Aylesford, and from this in Saxon times, daughter churches and chapels would be founded in scattered communities by priests from his church (Everitt, 1986). Within the vicinity of Ditton, St James' church, East Malling, originally called St Mary, and Birling Church were possibly mother churches which were followed by daughter churches. The church of St Mary and the chapel of St Leonard at West Malling, as well as a chapel at New Hythe might have been founded from East Malling. Other small daughter churches could have been established from the Aylesford Minster and known as *bookland churches* in Burham, and another by a stream settlement just a mile or so south-west of the mother church of St Peter, also called St Peter, at Ditton. Possibly to distinguish this church from the mother church and to reinforce a link with Rome, it was given the additional title of St Peter in Chains after the Basilica of St Peter in Vincoli in Rome that contains chains reputedly linked to the apostle St Peter. A *bookland church* was one erected on private land by a Saxon land owner (*thegn*), and shown to be his possession by a charter or *book*. Such churches had a burial ground, in contrast to field churches which were like chapels. A priest might travel from Aylesford to Ditton to take services in the church in exchange for various dues such as *tithe* (a tenth of crops), *churchscot* (a rate for the poor) and *soulscot* (burial fees).

The presence of churches in the Diocese of Rochester in late Saxon times is confirmed by a document, the *Textus Roffensis* which lists churches that paid money for chrism oil used in baptisms (Ward, 1932). A church paid 9 pence and a chapel 6 pence. In addition to Ditton (*Dictuna*), other local churches included

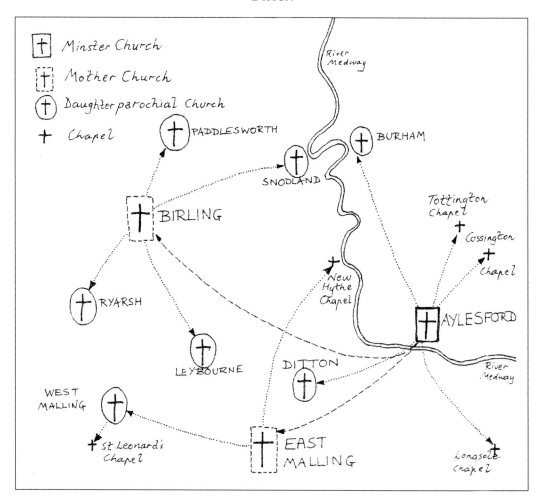

The possible progress of establishment of churches and chapels from the Aylesford Minster Church. Based on the work of Everitt, 1986

Aylesford (*Aeilesford*), East Malling (*Meallingis*), West Malling (*Meallingetes*), Leybourne (*Leleburna*), East Barming (*Bearmlinges*) and the chapel of St Leonard at West Malling. The presence of churches in these manorial communities is confirmed by their listing in the Domesday Book of 1086, although Aylesford church is overlooked (Page, 1932; Morris, 1983). After the Norman invasion in 1066, King William ordered a survey of the property of his kingdom; who owned the land in the time of Edward the Confessor (abbreviated to T.R.E. *Tempore Rex Edwardi*), the type of agricultural land, woodland, animals and the status of the inhabitants. Although the original Domesday text is written in an abbreviated form, it has been translated into modern English. The entry for Ditton is:

> Haimo the sheriff holds Dictune of the Bishop. It is assessed at 1 suling.
> There is land for 4 ploughs. On the demesne are 2 and 20 villeins with 5
> bordars and 3 ploughs. A church is there and 6 serfs and 1 mill worth 10

shillings and 8 acres of meadow and 35 acres of pasture and woodland for 6 pigs T.R.E. it was worth 8 pounds, when received 100 shillings. Now it is worth 8 pounds. Esbiorn held it of King Edward.

Haimo ten̄ de epo *DICTVNE* . p̄ uno ſolin ſe defd . Tra . ē

iiii . car̄ . In dn̄io ſunt . ii . 7 xx . uiƚƚi cū . v . bord hn̄t . iii . car̄.

Ibi æccƚa 7 vi . ſerui . 7 un̄ molin̄ de . x . ſolid . 7 viii . ac p̄ti.

7 xxx.v . ac paſturæ . Silua . vi . porc̄ . T . R . E :́ ualeb . viii.

ƚib . Q̇do recep̄:´ c . ſoƚ . Modo . viii . ƚib . Sbern tenuit

de rege . E.

A reproduction of the Domesday Book entry for DICTUNE (Ditton), from a facsimile edition of Abraham Furley, 1783

The Bishop who held Ditton was Odo Bishop of Bayeux, the first lord of the manor about whom we know anything, and this is not particularly flattering! He was a half brother of King William, having the same mother Herleva of Falaise, and his father was Viscount de Conteville. He was made a Bishop in 1049 when he was only 19 and had a reputation for being arrogant, greedy and very ambitious. He was a leading campaigner in the conquest of England, and as a consequence he was made Earl of Kent, and given around half of the four hundred or so manors in the county. In addition to Ditton, these included the local manors of Allington, Tottington, Eccles, Burham, Leybourne, Birling, Ryarsh, Offham and Addington. There is good evidence that he commissioned the Bayeux Tapestry on which he is represented four times. Eventually he fell out of favour with William, fought against William (Rufus) II, and died on a Crusade at Palermo in Sicily in 1097. Odo did not own some of the immediately local manors; Aylesford was held by King William, East Malling by the Archbishop of Canterbury, and West Malling by Bishop of Rochester. Odo had tried to appropriate the manor of West Malling among others, but was prevented from doing so by a shire court at Penenden Heath. One other manor which Odo held was called *Sifletone/Siffleton*, described as *in Ditton*.

The Domesday Book entry is:

Vitalis holds of the Bishop Sifleton. It is assessed as 3 yokes. There is land for one plough. On the demesne are one and a half ploughs and 6 villeins with 1 bordar and half a plough. There are 6 serfs and 1 mill worth 10 shillings.

There are 10 acres of meadow and 30 acres of pasture. T.R.E. it was worth 40 shillings, when received 4 pounds. Now it is worth 100 shillings, This land T.R.E. 2 men held in parage, Lewin and Ulwin and they could go to what lord they wished with their land.

These Domesday Book entries give a coded picture of Dictune in the middle of the 11th century. Located near the church was the Lord's farm (to become Ditton Court) with the stream nearby to drive the mill. The farm land of 1 sulung was about two hundred acres and required four eight-ox plough teams, while a further one hundred and fifty or so acres were in the lord's demesne. Altogether there were 33 workers varying from villeins to the more servile bordars to the even more controlled, serfs. It is likely that each worker had his own small wooden cottage as the term *bordar* is from the French word *borde* for a wooden hut. One can imagine that these small dwellings would be around the area of what is today the Green, the Stream, Ditton Place and Cobdown. The variety of land for crops (plough land), animals (pasture) and hay (meadow), would support a mixed farm, and the larger area of plough land would enable a third to be kept fallow for a year. One can envisage the plough lands stretching towards the present day Kiln Barn, and adjoining the extensive and essential woodland on the rising land towards Barming where in autumn pigs would be living on acorns. The tax payable to the lord of the manor for this was called *pannage*.

The exact location of the manor of *Sifleton*, which was either whole or in part joined to the manor of *Dictune* to form the parish of Ditton, is uncertain. Some distinctive features in the Domesday account such as the presence of a mill, but no church or woodland, would indicate land to the north of the village around the future Mill Hall Mill and Mill Hall (the manor hall?). It is possible that Sifleton was one of a number of hamlets in the large Saxon estate of Aylesford, which became a separate Domesday manor like Tottington, but was eventually linked in parochial organisation to both Ditton and Aylesford. A document from the 1360s refers to 'The manor of Syffleton in Aylesford and Ditton including a wharfe at Melhale on the water called the Medeway'. Like Ditton, *Sifleton* had some arable land for two and a half ploughs, and also meadow and pasture. Thus the joint manor of Ditton with part of Sifleton would have provided a well balanced parish of riverside meadows, extensive arable land and the potential use of two water mills, as well as an extensive tract of woodland. The name *Sifleton* vanished in Medieval times, and its origin and meaning are unknown. Perhaps it was a particular place where hay was made, as the Old English words *filethe-ton* describe. It was a well established farming practice in Kent to exploit water meadows near rivers, such as here near the Medway, especially for hay production.

There was much woodland on the Chart Hills and North Downs in Saxon and Norman times as there is still today. The lack of woodland in the manor of Sifleton, because of its geographical position, was a unique deficiency of manors in this immediate area. Ditton had wood for six pigs, East Malling for 60, West Malling 20, Leybourne 70, Aylesford 70, Tottington 2 and Eccles 10. The large and surprising area of woodland for Leybourne is explained by the relatively widespread Kentish custom of attaching a separate woodland to a manor. This is south of Offham, and is still called Leybourne Wood. West Malling had additional detached woodland near Blue Bell Hill, still known as Malling Wood. Aylesford also had detached woodland portions, at Rugmer Hill near Brenchley, and part of Mereworth Woods, where later a chapel was erected and dedicated to St Blaise. This is now a ruin near Blaze Wood (Everitt, 1986).

Although Odo, Bishop of Bayeux was the Lord of the Manor of both Ditton and *Sifleton*, these two manors had been in separate ownership before the Norman Conquest. Esbiorn owned Ditton (as well as Birling) and *Sifleton* was shared (called *parage* in the Domesday Book) between Lewin and Ulwin. With the transference of all property to King William, and from him to his relatives and favourites such as Odo, local manorial supervision of Ditton passed to Haimo (Hamo) the Sherriff (*shire-reeve*, the chief official) of Kent. In this vicinity he also had the oversight of the manors of Mereworth and Nettlestead. *Sifleton* was held from Odo by a Norman Knight called *Vitalis* (also known as *Vital* or *Viel*). He also had extensive land in Canterbury and was responsible for shipping stone from Caen to England, and is one of only two French Knights depicted on the Bayeux Tapestry.

Bishop Odo (ODO:EPS) with his half brothers, William the Conqueror (WILLELM) and Robert of Mortman (ROTBERT) as depicted in the Bayeux Tapestry when completed in 1077

It is likely that at the time of the Norman Conquest the small church at Ditton was constructed of wood as many were at this time, although evidence is now suggesting that many more were built of stone than originally thought. Saxon stone work is found in the local churches of Wouldham and West Peckham. A great rebuilding of churches with stone might well have followed the appointment of the former French monk, Gundulf, as Bishop of in 1077. He was then the most important builder in England, and was responsible for the White Tower in the Tower of London, Rochester Castle and considerable work in the cathedral, including the establishment of a Benedictine priory there. In his own manor of West Malling, then known as Little Malling (*Mellinges Parva*), he rebuilt St Mary's Church, constructed St Leonard's Tower near St. Leonard's chapel, and in 1090 established a Benedictine nunnery (Oakley, 1990). The consequence of these developments was that West Malling became a market town (Town Malling) and eclipsed East Malling in importance. The chancel and nave of Ditton Church were rebuilt in around 1100 with walls two to three feet thick, and although all windows and the roof have subsequently been changed, a contemporary blocked doorway still remains on the north side of the chancel. This would have been for the priest alone. The windows would have been very small, approximately six inches wide and 18 inches high, with three or four for the nave and only one at the east end of the chancel (Berg and Jones, 2009). Prior to rebuilding, the previous stone or wooden church might have been approximately the size of the present chancel. Norman rebuilding often enlarged churches by about 300%, but the new nave at Ditton of about thirty square metres would have been adequate for the population (Livett, 1893). Many other local churches, such as Aylesford, East Malling, West Malling, Leybourne, Ryarsh, Offham, Addington, Trottiscliffe and West Farleigh also have Norman work remaining. The Norman desire to rebuild churches and cathedrals and to establish many new monastic houses was in part in gratitude for the papal blessing on William's campaign and conquest. The importance of the new monastic developments will be discussed in the next chapter.

By the end of Norman rule, with the arrival of the Plantagenet King Henry II in 1154, the manors of Ditton and perhaps the whole or part of the manor of *Sifleton* had been united into the one ecclesiastical parish within boundaries that are very similar to those of Ditton today. It would by then have had a resident priest, supported by the tithe from land which was about one half arable, a quarter meadow and pasture, and a quarter woodland. Although we have no names of priests recorded until Adam in 1317, we know from papal legislation of 1108 that they had to be unmarried. Once established as a parish, the population is likely to have changed very little for the next eight hundred years. Added together Ditton and Sifleton had 45 men recorded in the Domesday Book. If

The external chancel wall of St Peter's Church showing Norman herringbone masonry

*Vitalis, also known as Vital who held the tenancy of the manor
of Sifleton from Bishop Odo. From the Bayeux Tapestry.*

these represent one man in family groups of two, three or four, and allowing for some of *Sifleton* being incorporated into Aylesford, there could well have been a population of between one hundred and one hundred and fifty. At the first census of Ditton in 1801 the population was only 98, however, in 1348-52 the Black Death reduced the population of England by about 30-40%, and it took many centuries to recover.

Incorporated into the parish of Ditton from late Norman times, was the so-called 'appendant Manor of Bram[p]ton'. Although there is no mention of this manor in the Domesday Book, it seems to refer to land to the east of St James' Church at East Malling. A rental of the Manor of East Malling in 1410 refers to land called *Bramtongate,* and a map of the same manor in 1706 names a field *Bramton* near the present East Malling Reseach Station (Williams, 1979).

Outside the parish, Ditton had a responsibility for the upkeep of bridge. Along with Wrotham, Maidstone, Wateringbury, Nettlestead, East and West Peckham, Mereworth and its manor of Swanton, Leybourne, Offham and Hadlow, it was allocated the maintenance of the fifth pier. Rochester bridge was a vital link on the line of communication across Kent which the followed the Roman road, Watling Street, from Dover and Canterbury to London. A wooden, and apparently precarious bridge with seven piers existed across the wide River Medway between 960-1387. A stone bridge that replaced it lasted until 1856. If the bridge was impassable, the alternatives were a ferry, or a longish journey to the lowest ford on the river at Aylesford, and then a journey on to London through Ditton.

Rochester Bridge from a late 18th century print. Ditton, with other parishes, was responsible for the maintenance of the fifth pier.

Chapter 4

Medieval Times: Church and Monastic Influence, 1154-1530

This abbot then, who was a holy man as abbots are, or else they ought to be.

The Canterbury Tales: Geoffrey Chaucer, 1342-1400

The relative stability that came to England with the reign of Henry I (1100-1135), the youngest son of William I, coincided with a period of revival in religious life throughout Europe. Many new monastic houses were built, and new orders such as the Cluniacs and Cistercians were established. Apart from the city of Canterbury, probably no other part of Kent had such a concentration of monastic houses and associated estates as Ditton and area (Page, 1926; Knowles and Hadcock, 1971). As mentioned above, in around 1090 Bishop Gundulf of Rochester founded a Benedictine nunnery at West Malling just two miles west of Ditton, and a few years later Gundulf's friend, Anselm, the Archbishop of Canterbury from 1093-1109, gave his manor of the adjacent parish of East Malling to Malling Abbey. In 1119 Robert de Crevecoeur of the family who built Leeds Castle, founded a priory for Augustinian Canons nearby, eight or so miles east of Ditton, which would have a more direct effect upon the parish. William Fitzhamo, the grandson of Vitalis lord of the manor of Sifleton at the time of Domesday, in 1142 granted to the Priory of Leeds the advowson (the right to appoint the rector, also known as the patronage) of Ditton. He did this for the health of his own soul and those of himself, and of his wife, his sons and his father and mother (MacMichael, 1962. Jessup 1956). Within a few years Leeds Priory had also been granted rectorial tithes of corn, hay and wood, and the responsibility for the maintenance of the chancel. The priest of Ditton then became a vicar, (from vicarius, a deputy) and received only the lesser tithes from minor crops. In addition the vicar of Ditton had to give the priory an annual gift of a bezant, a coin with a value then of two shillings. Just three or so miles to the north east of Ditton, William of Ypres founded a Cistercian abbey at Boxley in 1143 which subsequently owned a small piece of land in Ditton. Even nearer to Ditton, Sir Richard de Grey founded a Carmelite Friary at Aylesford in 1242 (Braun, 1950. McGreal, 1998). The de Grey family had obtained the royal manor of Aylesford in 1220. Sir Richard had become aware of the plight of persecuted Carmelites from Mount Carmel when fighting on the fifth Crusade in the Holy Land, and they were offered a home on his estate in Aylesford. Initially they were short of money, but an incentive was given by the Bishop of Rochester of 30 days' relief from penance if money was given for the church, and all who attended its dedication in 1248 were granted 40 days of indulgences.

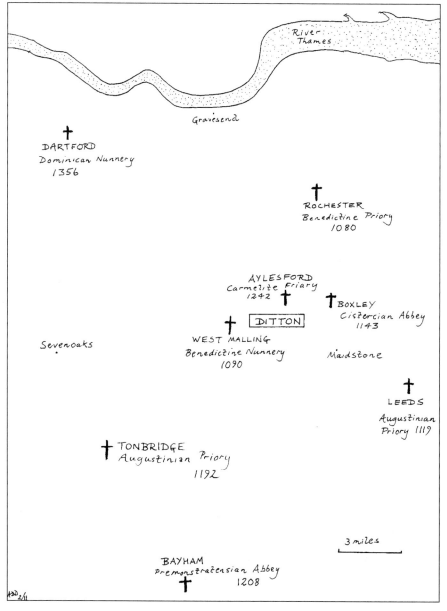

The location of monastic houses in mid- and west Kent in relation to Ditton,
with the date of their foundation

In addition to the establishment of religious houses, a number of small chapels were built within the vicinity of Ditton in the large parishes of East Malling and Aylesford. At New Hythe near the River Medway, there was a chapel dedicated to St John the Baptist (not on the site of the 1854 Holy Trinity Church) within East Malling parish. In Aylesford parish there were chapels at Tottington dedicated to St Stephen, at Cossington to St Michael, and at Longsole in the present day Hermitage Lane a remote chapel (a hermitage?) dedicated to St Lawrence. The dedications to St John the Baptist and St Lawrence were often used in medieval times for remote places of worship, and would be most appropriate in these instances (Everitt, 1986). For the residents of Ditton in the 12th and 13th centuries, the church of St. Peter, even at that time without a tower, would have seemed magnificent in size and quality. The inside would have been quite dark with a narrow chancel arch and relatively small, single light windows as still shown in the contemporary, but smaller churches of Dode and of St Benedict at Paddlesworth, and the chancels of St Margaret, Barming, and St Rumbold, Bonnington (Berg and Jones, 2009). The presence of the 'church' was thus very apparent in the lives of all village residents even when they went to the weekly markets on Wednesday and Saturday at West Malling. This had a market cross in the High Street, and they might have passed the Hundred Cross at Larkfield with an image the Virgin Mary, and another wayside cross or wayside shrine at Couch Green. Couch (Crouch) is derived from the latin crucis, a cross.

After the disgrace of Odo, Bishop of Bayeux, the lord of the manor of Ditton and Sifleton in 1095, the lordship passed to Richard de Clare, also known as Richard Fitzgilbert or Richard de Tonbridge (Wadmore, 1886). He, like almost all landowners after the Norman Conquest, was of Norman origin, and had been given extensive other estates throughout England, including the Manor of Clare in Suffolk from which he took his name. Locally the de Clare family were responsible for the building of Tonbridge Castle and the founding of Tonbridge Priory for Augustinian Canons in 1192. They also built the gigantic Caerphilly Castle in Wales, sometime described as 'one of the truly great strongholds of medieval Europe.' Because of their vast estates throughout England and Wales the family had many baronial titles – including Earl of Clare, Gloucester and Hereford. It is as Earls of Gloucester that they appear in connection with Ditton records until after many generations and the death of Gilbert de Clare in 1314 at the Battle of Bannockburn without an heir, the lands and titles passed through his sister to a niece, Margaret, who married Lord Stafford. A record of 1362 refers to the holding of the manor of Syffleton in Ditton and Aylesford from the Earl of Stafford (Cal. of Inquisitions, 1362). Like all landed barons, the de Clares held estates from the reigning monarch on the condition of giving 40 days of military service each year to the king. One could be excused this service on the

Dode Curch, Luddesdown

St Peter's Church, Ditton

payment of a so-called knight's fee. Monastic or clerical holders of manors would be unable to give military service, and thus paid a fee. If a tenant died, in theory the land reverted to the crown, and a relief payment was made to take the land again, thus contributing more to the royal coffers! In this way money was raised by monarchs to enable them to fight wars. At the level of the individual manor, a tenant could hold land provided he gave appropriate feudal service. We know that in 1242 William de Ditton (also known as de Shoford) held land in Ditton from the Earl of Gloucester for half a fee. Two other parish landowners, William de Sifflatun and William de Bramton paid a quarter fee. This probably gives an indication of the relative size of their holdings, and a half fee would be military service for 20 days or an appropriate knight's fee. (Inq. Post Mortem, 1861) In 1262, Ralph de Ditton held Ditton, Sifflington and other estates from the Earl of Gloucester for three and a half fees. Within the village community the villeins, bordars and serfs would also give their feudal service to their immediate lord. This could involve the taking of arms, but was usually boon work on the Lord's demesne farm.

Ploughing in the 14th century as depicted in the Luttrell Psalter

The de Ditton family were descended from another Norman knight Vitalis, whose grandson William Fitzhamo had given the advowson of St. Peter's to Leeds Priory. At this time, before the stabilisation of surnames as we know them, naming was becomingly related to a father's name, and often linked to fitz (son of). For example the family line from Vitalis, also known as Viel, passed though Hamo Fitzviel to William Fitzhamo to Hamo Fitzwilliam. It is likely that at the beginning of the 12th century they became resident in Ditton, as the son of Hamo Fitzwilliam was called William de Soford or Shofford alias de Ditton (MacMichael, 1962). He was the father of Ralph de Ditton, mentioned above. Many family names at this time were linked to a place of residence, for example, the Twisden family of Bradbourne, who were to play an important part in the history of Ditton for nearly three hundred years, originated in the manor of Twyssenden in Goudhurst. The economic status of Ralph de Ditton and his son, also Ralph de Ditton, is shown by the Lay Subsidy of 1334 (Harley and Chalklin,

1964). This was a tax on property that was surplus to the subsistence living of households, and was raised to pay for territorial wars in France. The records for the Hundred of Larkfield list 297 individual names without giving the name of parishes. The largest fee of 10 shillings was paid by the Archdeacon of Rochester, and the majority of other payments were of two shillings or under. The Abbess of Malling Abbey paid 4s..8d, but one of the highest other payments was by Ralph de Ditton, who paid 6s..8d. This would indicate that Ralph lived in substantial style in a manor house, alias Ditton Court. He also had land in Offham, and was perhaps an increasingly prosperous farmer in the period before the trauma of the Black Death in 1348-9. By contrast to a relatively substantial manor house, the other significant buildings in the parish would have been the two watermills, but the dwellings of the labourers would have been of simple wood construction, with a bare earth floor and a thatched roof.

14th century additions to St Peter's Church: a. the piscina; b. a front of nave window

The beginning of the 14th century may well have been a period of relative prosperity in the parish. The first recorded rector, Adam dictus ad aquam Maydestone was appointed by Leeds Priory in 1317 and there were major changes to St.Peter's church. On the inside south wall of the chancel a piscina was constructed for the priest to wash the mass vessels, and a new octagonal font was installed on a much older circular base. On both north and south sides of the front of the nave, two large two-light windows were inserted. Even today, these give the church a characteristic lightness, and in the north window there are some remnants of contemporary stained glass including an angel swinging an incense censor. The roofs of both nave and chancel were raised with a distinctive high pitched braced oak construction, possibly made from oak grown in the parish. Unlike the churches at Aylesford, and East and West Malling, St. Peter's Church at Ditton did not have a Norman tower. The construction of the present tower was commenced in the early 14th century, together with a large arch at the rear of the church to illuminate the west end of the nave (this is now obscured by the gallery and organ). The building of the tower might have taken many years to complete, as bequests and gifts became available, but ultimately it provided a proper place for a bell or bells to call people to worship, and to sound the moment of the elevation of the host at mass. The main door to the church was on the south side, and had a porch, used for marriages in medieval times. This door was blocked and the porch removed in the restoration of the 1850s.

The arrival of an outbreak of bubonic plague known as the Black Death in England in 1348 after some years of poor harvests, had a dire effect on virtually every community and institution, with a loss in some places of half of the population. The fact that three vicars of Ditton are recorded for the years between 1347 and 1356 suggests that there was a serious outbreak in the parish. Nearby at Malling Abbey, two abbesses died in one year, 1349. It is likely that the Black Death had a devastating effect on the de Ditton family who do not figure in records after this time. Thomas de Dyttone and Radulphus (Ralph) de Dyttone are mentioned in a Feudal Aid of 1347, when money was raised by Edward III at the time of the knighting of his eldest son, Edward the Black Prince (Greenstreet, 1876). It is possible that other major work at St.Peter's Church. such as an enlargement of all the nave windows was put on hold, and in fact did not occur until the mid 19th century. The Black Death also had a profound effect on feudal obligations. Because of the death of so many labourers, those who remained could bargain for their services, and the old feudal service obligations were now replaced by payment for labour. Labourers could also hold land from the lord of the manor, an agreement which was entered on a manor roll, a copy of which was given to the labourer. He thus became a copyholder. The shortage of labour meant that many cottagers moved to other manors to obtain better wages, but this was limited by the Statute of Labourers of 1351 which prevented movement between manors, and maintained wages at the level of 1348.

There was a great shortage of priests after the Black Death, and it might have been many years before adequate replacements were found. From Langland's writing in Piers Plowman in 1380 (Langland, 1966), we know that the standard of priest could be rather poor!

I have been priest and parson for thirty winters past,
But I cannot solfa or sing, or read a latin life of saints.
But I can find a hare in a field or in a furrow.
I can hold a friendly meeting, I can cast a shire's accounts,
But in a mass-book or Pope's edict I cannot read a line.

Simple Christian teaching was given by instruction through pictures in stained glass windows and in wall paintings. It is possible that under the whitewash of the St.Peter's nave walls, even today, there are pictures of St Christopher, the Passion, the Annunciation, the seven deadly sins and other didactic images, such as those from the 13th century still shown in the relatively local churches of St.Thomas of Canterbury at Capel near Tonbridge of Cain and Abel, and at St John the Baptist at Halling of the Last Supper and Christ's Passion (Rosewell, 2008). Reinforcing the Christian teaching which took place within St. Peter's church was the teaching and evangelistic work of the Carmelite Friars from Aylesford. After the uncertain beginnings of this monastic house in the 13th century, it gained considerable local support and popularity largely because of the presence and work of the brothers outside the Priory. Of all the monastic houses in West Kent, it received more bequests and gifts in the century or so before the Reformation than any other (Lees, 2001).

The communication links between Ditton and Aylesford, which had depended upon the state of the tide at the ford across the River Medway, were greatly improved by the construction of a wooden bridge. This is known to have been in existence in 1287 and would have been particularly useful for residents of Ditton

Aylesford Bridge over the River Medway. A photograph taken in 1927. This bridge was built in the 14th century and modified with a large central arch in 1824.

and other parishes to the south of the Medway for visiting the weekly Aylesford market which had been established in 1350. The present elegant stone bridge was constructed in the 1390s, although the two central arches were replaced in 1824 to allow the passage of larger craft to Maidstone and beyond. It still remains as one of the iconic sights of Kent.

It would seem that throughout the 14th and early 15th centuries the manor of Ditton with Sifleton and Bramton was a very small pawn in the hands of large and important landowners who probably hardly knew of its existence. In contrast the manor of East Malling was in local monastic hands, and remained unchanged in ownership from around 1100 to 1538. Ditton Court, the seat of local manorial government, was then probably the residence of a reeve who managed the estate. It was not until 1904, when Ditton Court Farm was sold by the Preston Hall estate to the tenant Thomas Scott, that for the first time in its long history it became an owner occupied farm. Names of owners that occur in records of Ditton from the 14th century include Sir Walter Pavely of Windsor, Lord Clifford of Clifford in Herefordshire, and then in 1472 Sir Richard Colepeper (Culpeper) of Oxenhoath in West Peckham. This famous Kentish family were to have various, but not continuous links with Ditton until 1734. The first recorded link of the Colepeper family with Ditton was 100 years earlier in 1372 when Walter Colepeper was the owner of Borough Court in the north of the parish. The manor farmhouse of Borough Court was demolished in the 1920s, and was reputed to be 'of great age,' and could have been roughly contemporary with the so-called Wealden Hall a mile or so south in Larkfield, dating from around 1350. After acquiring the manor of Ditton in 1472 as well as the manor of Borough Court by inheritance, Sir Richard Colepeper became the owner of the entire parish of Ditton. This was probably the last time in history that the entire parish was under one owner. On his death in 1484 one of his three daughters, Elizabeth, who was married to Henry Barham of Teston, inherited the manor of Ditton, and sold Borough Court to the Lancastrian Shakerley family, who were to own it for well over 150 years.

The excellence of much of the local agricultural land together with the proximity of an ever expanding market in the metropolis of London, with good links for products by water from the nearby inland 'ports' of New Hythe and Mill Hall indicates a time of increased prosperity among the landowners of Kent. This is shown by the high quality and number of Wealden hall-type farmhouses built in this area in the 14th and 15th centuries. The Wealden Hall at Larkfield has already been mentioned, and is not only one of the earliest timber halls in existence, but also one of the largest. Stream Cottage in Ditton was built in around 1420-30, although the solar wing was added at around 1480-1500. Almost contemporary local hall houses still exist in Church Walk, and near Springhead in East Malling, and in St. Leonard's Street in West Malling.

Stream Cottage, built as a hall-house in around 1420-30. The hall, with a central fire, would have been in the central section. Subsequent modifications have included the addition of fireplaces and chimneys and a floor at first floor level in the hall. The nearest wing was added or modified between 1480-1500. An additional wing was added in the late 20th century.

While such building developments were taking place, there was a major addition to the furnishings of St.Peter's Church. It became almost universal in English churches at the end of the 15th century to set up a screen at the front of the nave with an effigy of the crucified Christ, with one of St.Mary on one side and St John on the other. The name rood screen is derived from the old English word for 'cross,' rood. We know that money was left for the construction and painting of the rood loft in Burham beteen 1498 and 1516, and for painting the rood loft in Aylesford in 1524. In St.Peter's church the screen was erected to the west of the two large windows and not adjacent to the chancel arch, a situation repeated in the churches of both East and West Malling. Access to the top of the screen for decoration, to light lamps and perhaps for music was provided by a small staircase built into the south wall of the nave. Although this screen like most others has totally vanished, the entrance to the rood stairs is still evident. Stairs

---

Opposite: The Old Mill House, the house of Church Mill. Built as a timber house in the late 16th century without a central hall, but with integral fireplaces and chimneys.
Top. Around 1905; Centre. In 1942; Bottom. Early 21st century after major restoration.

in an external turret are still to be seen at Aylesford, and a rare local example of a complete screen, without figures, remains in the church at Shoreham in the Darenth valley. The maintenance of a parish church was an important feature of medieval wills, and we know that an Elyanor Aldressh left money for the purchase of shingles for the repair of St Peter's roof in 1513. The vicar of Ditton at the end of the 15th century, Hugh Hudson, requested in his will in 1501 'to be buried in the choir within the church' (the chancel), and also left over £3 for the repair of the church porch. In a rather unusual bequest, he left to his successor, Laurence Skoye his best portoise on condition that he did not ask for more money for the repair of the parsonage house. A portoise was a book of psalms, hymns and prayers, more usually known as a Breviary. Furthermore he left the church a ' a quire containing the story of our lady called The Visitation.' This would have been a devotional book concerning the visit of the Virgin Mary to her cousin Elizabeth (Duncan, 1906). Although we have no memorial to Hugh Hudson, there is still remaining a small brass plate in the chancel commemorating Richard Leggatt who died on the 6th June 1481.

The Visitation of the Virgin Mary to her cousin Elizabeth, from a Book of Hours *of 1519.*

While 15th and early 16th century developments in church furnishing were taking place, there was an undercurrent of religious reform that would lead eventually to the Reformation. Lollardy, especially associated with teachings of John Wycliffe (1330-1384) had many followers in Kent, particularly in the Wealden areas. Later some followers of William Tyndale were burnt at the stake. These included John Hitton a joiner of Maidstone in 1530, and John Frith of Westerham in 1533. The vicar of Ditton in 1532, John Bechynge, was sympathetic to the cause of these reformers, and stated in contrast to the accepted teachings of the time, that there was no scriptural basis for confession to a priest (Zell, 2000). Although he subsequently recanted his opinions, it was only a few years before there was a complete break with the pope and the Church of Rome. This led to the dissolution of the monasteries and a vast change in land ownership on a scale unprecedented since the Norman Conquest, and major practical and theological changes to all churches throughout England.

A chapter heading drawing of an unnamed church in Old Country Life *by S. Baring-Gould, published in 1895. The drawing by F.D. Bedford is of Ditton Church with Ditton Court in the background (compare with the picture on page 42).*

Chapter 5

The Reformation to the Restoration: 1530-1660

Laws and statutes of this realm made for the abolishing of the Bishop of Rome's pretensed and usurped power and jurisdiction within this realm, and for the establishment of the king's authority.

Royal Injunction 1536

Many people living in Ditton through the 1530s and 40s and working on the varied agricultural land, or in the woods and corn mills, would probably been relatively unaware of the major national events that were unfolding. They would have met together with all social classes of the parish in Sunday celebrations of the Latin mass, and on special holy days in St. Peter's Church. They would have been unable to contribute much to the upkeep of the church or to the small tithes to support the vicar, or the more extensive great tithes that went to the Augustinian Priory at Leeds, but would have been aware of the collection of a tenth of the crops each year.

Henry VIII, by an Act of Supremacy in 1534, made himself head of the Church of England, *Anglicana Ecclesia* (Gee and Hardy, 1896). Among other well-known disagreements with Rome concerning his marriage, he had become increasingly concerned at the amount of church revenue that went straight to the Vatican. He instigated a national survey of the value of church and monastic property, known as the *Valor Ecclesiasticus*, which was completed in 1535 (Carly and Hunter, 1810).   At this time, when Thomas Kempe was vicar of Ditton, his income was valued at just under £12 per annum. This was a reasonable financial reward as the local livings of Addington, Allington, Birling, Offham and Ryarsh were only valued between £6and £8. The nearby Malling Abbey was valued after deductions at £218, while Leeds Priory, one of the most wealthy in Kent, at £362. A tenth of these amounts was now diverted to the crown; this was a prelude to the appropriation of all monastic property. The closure of monastic houses, known as the Dissolution of the Monasteries, commenced in 1536. The nearby monastic houses of Malling, Aylesford and Boxley were closed in 1538, and Leeds Priory in around 1540. The Crown claimed ownership of these former monastic properties and their extensive estates, and thus, over the next few years there was the greatest redistribution of land ownership throughout England since the Norman Conquest.

The buildings of Malling Abbey in 1724. On the right the Great Tower is linked to the ruined nave of the church. The building on the left of the quadrangle is a first floor refectory with the still existent cloister below (see Oakley, 1990). A large house was built on the site in 1746.

Some of the buildings of Malling Abbey were converted into a private house, but were returned to monastic use in 1892 as an order of Anglican Benedictine Nuns. The Manor of East Malling, formerly part of Malling Abbey estates, was purchased in 1657 by Thomas Twisden of Bradbourne House, East Malling. He and his descendants would have a major influence on Ditton for nearly 300 years. Some of the Carmelite Friary at Aylesford was demolished, and after brief ownership by Sir Thomas Wyatt of Allington Castle, passed after his execution (see below) to the Crown, and then in 1570 to John Sedley. This family endowed the Hospital of the Holy Trinity (almshouses) in Aylesford in 1605. Following ownership by the Rycaut and Banks families, the Friars became the home of the Finch family in 1699. Heneage Finch who was created Earl of Aylesford in 1719, obtained the advowson (the right to appoint the incumbent) of St. Peter's Church Ditton, and it was held by this family until 1899. What was left of the old Friary buildings after demolition, re-building and fire, was returned to monastic use in 1949 with the arrival of the Carmelites Friars. The Manor of Leybourne, including the castle, had been owned by a Cistercian monastery, the Abbey of St. Mary of Graces in London from 1350 to1538. Eventually a mansion house was built on the site of a monastic farm (a grange), familiar in the 20th century as an isolation hospital. This redistribution of land and property thus brought many new land owners into this part of mid Kent, joining others such as the long established Colepeper who continued to reside at Preston Hall until the death of Alicia Milner (nee Colepeper) in 1734.

In parallel with these changes to the monasteries and their property, each parish church saw some major events in the next twenty years. When Thomas Kempe was vicar of Ditton, extensive Royal Injunctions in 1538 instigated by the Lord Chancellor, Thomas Cromwell, requested that a large English Bible should be purchased for the church. This was the so-called Great Bible, and was to be paid for half and half by parson and parishioners and to be freely available for all to read. A register book was to be commenced 'wherein ye shall write the day and year of every wedding, christening, and burying within your parish.' The earliest Ditton registers have vanished apart from a few records for the years 1567-1598, but are extant continuously from 1663. In 1549, in the early years of Edward VIs reign, the rood loft across the front of the nave was taken down, wall paintings were whitewashed over, the stone altar was replaced with a wooden table, and an English Book of Common Prayer was introduced. For the first time all villagers could participate in worship in their own tongue led by the then rector, Nicholas Archebolde. It is likely that he was married as he ceased to be the vicar in 1553, the year that Queen Mary came to the throne and reintroduced Roman Catholic worship, reaffirming the practice of priestly celibacy. Hundreds of married priests, including those of nearby East Malling and Teston, and some bishops, were removed from their posts throughout the Church of England, leaving in some dioceses just about a fifth of incumbents. We have no idea how the parishioners of Ditton responded to these various changes, but many Kentish people resisted the return to Catholicism, and over sixty people, including some from Wrotham and Maidstone were burnt at the stake for not accepting these changes (Timpson, 1859). It is well-known that the Protestant cause had considerable support in the Weald, and possibly in this area of mid-Kent as demonstrated by support for Sir Thomas Wyatt, junior. The Wyatt family, from Yorkshire, came to Allington Castle in 1492, purchasing much land for their estate including some in Ditton in 1509. Sir Thomas Wyatt, senior (1503-1542), became a member of the court of King Henry, as well as a poet of considerable fame. Perhaps this Tudor noblemen and his son could be seen riding or hunting in the large tract of woodland that stretched from Allington to Oaken Wood and beyond. One of Thomas's poetic songs begins: (Rebholz,1978)

I must go walk the woods so wild
And wander here and there.

Sir Thomas Wyatt (senior)
1503-1542 of Allington Castle
by Hans Holbein the younger

His rather adventurous son, also Thomas, junior (1520-1554) was much concerned about the projected marriage of Queen Mary to Philip of Spain, and raised a force of men from mid-Kent in an attempt to overthrow the Queen and to re-establish a Protestant monarch. His mission failed, and he was executed on Tower Hill at the age of 34. However, Queen Mary did marry Philip, but died childless in 1558, and her half-sister, Elizabeth became Queen of England. The Book of Common Prayer was re-introduced with some modifications into each parish church, where it is still found more than 450 years later, with a preface authorised by Primo Elizabethae.

As the advowson of Ditton and its rectorial tithes had been held by Leeds Priory until 1540, they then reverted to the crown. At some point the status of the incumbent of Ditton changed from vicar to rector. This might have been a recognition of the fact that the vicarial (lesser) tithes were too small to support a married parish priest! A condition of this status was that the rector had to maintain the chancel. The advowson of Ditton passed in Elizabeth I's reign to the Shakerley family of Borough Court. This family of lawyers had come to Kent from Lancashire in the 1480s. The only physical reminder of their presence in Ditton is the remnant of a brass memorial to Rowland Shakerley who died in 1576, in the chancel of St Peter's Church. Most of this monument has been removed, apart from the feet and an inscription: 'this memorial of his death made by a young gentlewoman as an argument of her unseparable good meaning towards him'. His brother, Peter was charged at Maidstone Assizes in 1582 with assaulting Thomas Burnett, a smith of East Malling. A few years later in 1591, George Playce, a labourer from Maidstone stole three goslings and a belt from Francis Shakerley.

His punishment was a whipping (Cockburn, 1979). A stone floor monument now no longer visible, recorded the death of Elizabeth Shakerley late wife of Richard Shakerley of Ditton Esquire died 17th February Anno 1626. Lawyers were one of the few recognised professions in Tudor England, and perhaps the Shakerley family had come south to be within easy distance of London where training took place at Inns of Court and Chancery. There were good career prospects and major employment in the courts at Westminster and numerous other posts as treasurers, land agents and town clerks. Many aspiring families took up residence within striking distance of London, the number diminishing the further from the capital.

Remains of a brass memorial in St Peter's Church to Rowland Shakerley who died in 1576

At the end of the 16th century the Brewer family came to live in Ditton place, where they remained for over a hundred years. Like the Shakerley family of Borough Court they were landowners and lawyers. In emulating other aspiring Tudor families they probably converted a smallish timber framed farmhouse into a comfortable brick residence. A fireplace was now an important feature of houses, replacing the open hearth in the centre of a hall house of the earlier years, as in Stream Cottage. Its location by the stream with grounds rising attractively towards Bradbourne Lane, and with farm attached, made Ditton Place the largest private house in the parish. Richard Brewer, who died in 1616, is described as 'gentleman' on his stone floor memorial in the chancel of St. Peter's. There are at least 12 other floor memorials to the next three generations of the Brewer family, some in Latin such as that to the lawyer 'Guilielmi Brewer, de Gray's Inn' who died in 1657. William Brewer was for many years a member of the Grand Jury at the Maidstone Assizes together with other Kentish landowners. This socially upper middle ranking family married into the those of a similar strata of Kentish society from Acrise, Hadlow and Addington. One of the finest hanging memorials in Ditton Church is in Latin, with the Brewer family coat of arms. It records Richard Brewer who died in 1672, and his two wives and children. It was erected by his eldest son Thomas, who with pleasure placed this marble as a monument well-deserved to the memory of his parents, and of his own grateful feelings. An indication of the economic status of the Brewer family is provided by the Kent Assizes in Maidstone in 1634. Edward Harris of Ditton, described as a labourer, was brought to court and charged with burglary from William Brewer. He stole five silver spoons, nine pewter dishes, three pewter porringers, six ells of cloth, a meal bag, a brass skillet, a brass pot, a pepper box and a pewter salt cellar. The severity of punishment was usually increased if the items were taken for personal gain, as in this case, rather than subsistence for living. Harris was found guilty and punished by hanging (Cockburn, 1980).

Hanging memorial to members of the Brewer family of Ditton Place, circa 1691 (described by Newman, 1969 , as 'nearly top-quality')

At the end of the 15th century the Lordship of the Manor of Ditton with Sifleton (*Sifflynton*) and Brampton had been obtained by Henry Barham of Teston by marriage to Elizabeth Colepeper. After inheritance by his son Thomas Barham, the Manor of Ditton passed out of local ownership for around 100 years, until purchased by Sir Oliver Boteler a descendant of the Barham family. The subsequent owners of Lordship of the Manor of Ditton through this period were largely men at the centre of national government and royal power, and thus on hand to further their own cause. The Manor passed from Thomas Barham in 1509 to Sir Thomas Leigh of Lyminge in Kent. In 1547 the Leigh family exchanged the manor for other ex-monastic manors owned by the crown which were closer to Lyminge in East Kent. Close to the centre of Henry VIII's court was Sir Thomas Wriothesley (pronounced Risley) of Titchfield in Hampshire. Wriothesley has been described as the most successful civil servant of his day. Like many royal servants at that time, 'he put in his thumb and pulled out a plum' (a rhyme associated with the Horner family of Somerset in similar circumstances) and acquired along with the Manor of Ditton former monastic houses and manors in eight counties of England as well as three houses and a manor in London, and was given the title of Earl of Southhampton. This Earl's grandson Henry Wriothesley, was the chief patron of William Shakespeare, and a dedicatee of much of his poetry. He, however, did not inherit the Manor of Ditton as it had passed briefly to Sir Thomas Southwell M.P., a lawyer who handled the revenue from the dissolution of the monasteries. He was married to Margaret Neville from Mereworth. In 1554 the manor was purchased by Sir Thomas Pope from Oxfordshire. His interest in this small Kentish manor must have been rather slight as he owned 27 other manors in seven counties. He was a another civil servant who was entrusted with the guardianship of Princess Elizabeth, the future queen. Sir Thomas Pope is especially well-known as the founder of Trinity College Oxford, formed from the erstwhile Durham College. After Sir Thomas Pope's death in 1559, the Manor of Ditton was owned by the Wiseman family until a return to the local ownership of Sir Oliver Boteler of Teston in 1610. Boteler came from Bedfordshire and married Anne Barham, the heiress of Barham Court and the Teston estates in 1604, and was knighted in the same year.

Although the title Lord of the Manor had considerable significance from Norman times, ever since the Black Death in the 14th century its powers were diminishing. Although the lordship of Ditton was held by non-residents, the Manor Court would have continued to meet far less frequently than the medieval three times a week, if at all. Tenants of Ditton Court Farm would pay a fixed rent with tenancy agreements about things such as building maintenance and care of land and field boundaries. Within the parish a new form of local government, the Vestry, was emerging, which was to hold sway until major reforms of the 1830s. With the

Sir Thomas Wriothesley (1505-1550) first Earl of Southampton and Lord of the Manor of Ditton, by Hans Holbein the younger

dissolution of the monasteries, some of the philanthropic and caring works that were part of their purpose came to an end. However the Injunctions of Elizabeth I in 1559 ordered that every church was to have an alms chest to the intent the parishioners should put into it their oblations and alms for their poor neighbours' (Gee and Hardy, 1896). Many individuals left specific bequests for the poor; for example, Richard Burnet of East Malling left money in 1578 to give wheat to poor people of the parish, and in Aylesford John Sedley left money in 1605 to 'build houses for six poor aged and impotent persons.' Although both of these parishes had a number of later charitable gifts, and Ditton had its first from Thomas Golding in 1705, national legislation of 1601 had made each parish legally responsible for its own poor and needy. A Poor Rate was raised on all property in the parish, and distributed as appropriate by parish officers called the Overseers of the Poor who worked with the two churchwardens whose office can be traced back as far as 1127. Other officers were the Waywardens, or Surveyors of Highways who were first appointed after national legislation in 1555. Every cottager or householder had to work on the roads for six days each year, and each farmer had to provide a cart with two men for four days each year, working under the direction of the Waywarden. The Parish Constables, often called Borsholders in Kent, were officers of manorial government, but evolved to become parish officers responsible for law and order under the authority of the magistrates. These officers together ran the parish 'welfare state' through the regular meetings of the Vestry, which met in the vestry of the parish church. We know more about the work of the churchwardens from a later period as their Account Book exists from 1677 and of the Overseers of the Poor whose account book dates from 1731. These will be discussed in the next chapter. The Constables and Waywardens of Ditton must have had a particularly taxing time in the 1630s by the behaviour of a farmer (husbandman) of Ditton, William Burges. On a number of occasions he was taken to the local magistrates and on to the County Assizes in Maidstone for 'erecting two gates and posts in the highway between Ditton and Barming', and for 'blocking the highway leading from Ditton to Aylesford with posts and rails' and for 'depositing dung and soil in the highway of Ditton Green.' (Cockburn, 1980).

Two features which contributed to the prosperity of this part of Mid-Kent in the 16th and 17th centuries, were good river access to the expanding Metropolis of London and productive agricultural land. The 'inland ports' of New Hythe and Mill Hall, both on the edge of Ditton, were becoming increasingly busy. In the 1580s much wheat was shipped to London from Kent and timber for the dockyard at Chatham (then the most important naval dockyard in England), and iron products from the Wealden ironworks of places such as Lamberhurst and Brenchley were brought overland to Mill Hall for shipment to London. The River Medway was only navigable above Maidstone from 1740. Ragstone, Fuller's Earth and some sand were also shipped away. Imports were brought to these inland ports as well, and we know that a cargo of pepper destined for Wrotham was seized by customs in Rochester in 1601. A number of men who lived in New Hythe were identified as hoyman, shipwright, waterman or sailmaker.

New initiatives in farming in the 16th century were to change Kentish agriculture for good and alter the appearance of Ditton to this day with orchards and (now unused) oast houses. Some of the first commercially developed orchards in Kent date from around the 1530s, and hops from later in that century. Hop-gardens developed from a few acres to fields of thirty or more acres in the 17th century. Ditton parish, with around a third of its area as coppice woodland with oak standards, was in a good position to provide hop poles and fencing. Perhaps some flax was grown on the farms of Ditton at this time for the developing thread trade for which Maidstone became famous.

After the bewildering changes within all English parish churches between the 1530s and 1560, the reign of Elizabeth I heralded a period of relative national stability, increasing prosperity, and international expansion. In 1569, with the threat of possible invasion, every parish in each Hundred had to enlist men between the ages of 18 and 46 to form part of a local Muster. This threat of invasion eventually passed with the destruction of the Spanish Armada in 1587. When Elizabeth died in 1603 the heir to the Bradbourne estate, John Manningham, wrote delightfully in his diary: 'hir Majestie departed this lyfe, mildly like a lambe, easily like a ripe apple from the tree. I thinke the sorrowe for hir Majesties departure was soe deep in many hearts they could not soe suddenly shewe anie great joy.' (Sorlien, 1976). Through the reign of 45 years Ditton had had four rectors. George Attke who was appointed in Mary's reign in 1554, must have happily accepted the change from Catholic to Protestant practices in the church, as he remained rector until 1565. He would have lived in the rectory in Kiln Barn Road. It had extensive land and more glebe land around the parish. We know that the building was thatched, and that water was provided by a well. It is now the site of Cherry Orchard. William Prewe, who was rector from 1608 to 1638 is the first to have had a memorial in St Peter's Church. It has a Latin inscription that is now partially obscured, and records that *Guilielmi Prewe hujus que ecclesiae rectoris fidlissimi* (William Prewe a most faithful rector of this church). As well as his faithful ministry in the parish, he was probably on good social terms with the local and neighbouring landowners. He, with Richard Brewer of Ditton Place were witnesses to the will of Richard Manninhgam of Bradbourne House. Richard died in April 1611, leaving the Bradbourne estate to John Manningham a lawyer and diarist (see above), who was the grandson of his brother. John, in turn left the moated house of Bradbourne to his own son Richard, who sold it to Thomas Twisden (1602-1682) in 1657. He changed the spelling of his name to distinguish his family line from that of the Twysdens of Royden Hall, East Peckham. (Twisden, 1939)

Thomas Twisden's brother, Sir Roger Twysden(1597-1672) is a good example of a wise and moderate Kentish lawyer, politician and landowner of the first half of the 17th century, who could see both sides of the problems between King and Parliament (Everitt, 1966. Melling, 1960). However, in Kent, as well as in many counties in England, Cavalier and Parliament sides became more polarised, and some conflict was inevitable. Of this more extreme type on the Royalist side was Sir William Boteler of Teston, the lord of the manor of Ditton, and owner of Ditton Court and much of Oaken Wood, and Sir Peter Rycaut of the Friars at Aylesford. For the moderates in Kent there were several causes for concern: the demands of ship money in 1635 to Charles I's navy, and the increasing emphasis on Anglo-Catholic practices in the Church of England by Archbishop Laud on the one hand, and the more anti-monarchy and increasingly more puritan element in the Long Parliament on the other. They met in the Spring Assizes in Maidstone in 1642 and sent The Kentish Petition for moderation and tolerance to Parliament. Some of the key figures in drafting the petition were arrested, and Parliament sent representatives to the next Maidstone Assizes. Now the more extreme Royalists such as Sir William Boteler and the poet Richard Lovelace created more opposition to Parliament about the petition, and were imprisoned. Lovelace's well-known poem 'To Althea, from Prison', recounts this experience, and his support for the monarchy.

When (like committed Linnets) I
With Shriller throat shall sing
The sweetness, Mercy, Majesty,
And glories of my KING;

Stone Walls doe not a Prison make,
Nor Iron bars a cage....

This prompted certain Royalist families such as the Rycauts of The Friars at Aylesford to assemble arms, but a Parliamentary force under Colonel Edwyn Sandys was dispatched to Kent to deal with them. Perhaps the ordinary people of Ditton were astonished to see Sandys and his troop of men turn from the London road to Aylesford at Ditton Corner where Sir Peter Rycaut was arrested and much of his valuable goods taken. Then they might have passed over the wooded hills of Oaken Wood to Barham Court at Teston where the steward of Sir William Boteler refused to give up plate and money. Sandy's troop then resorted to force, terrifying the servants, breaking down doors and opening trunks to find valuables, before marching down the Medway valley to take over Maidstone. The Parliamentary cause throughout England was financed by sequestration (taking) of Royalist property and estates. Sir William Boteler's Estate, including much of Ditton, was sequestered, but he was able to reclaim it by paying a sum of over £3000. This money was used specifically to pay for the garrison which held Dover Castle for Parliament. The Parliamentary Committee that governed Kent from 1643 met first at Knole in Sevenoaks, then from 1644 for two years at The Friars, Aylesford. Sir William Boteler, meanwhile, was trying to raise an army for the King but was killed at Cropredy Bridge near Banbury in a skirmish with a Parlimentry force. The Lordship of the Manor of Ditton then passed to his son Sir Oliver Boteler.

The relatively peaceful Parliamentary occupation of Kent was shattered by a major confrontation in Maidstone in 1648. Because there had been some opposition in Kent, Colonel Sir Thomas Fairfax, one of Cromwell's outstanding commanders was dispatched to Kent with and army of 4000 troops. As there was a rebel gathering in the Maidstone area, Fairfax and his men came from London over the North Downs near Ryarsh and camped on East Malling Heath on the edge of Oaken Wood. The rebels in Maidstone thought that the Parliamentary force would cross the Medway by either the Aylesford or Maidstone bridges. Fairfax sent a small troop from the Heath, possibly through Ditton, to Aylesford to mislead the rebels. He then crossed the Medway by the unguarded East Farleigh Bridge, and won a decisive battle in Maidstone on 1st June, 1648.

With the execution of King Charles I in 1649, and the death of the Lord

Protector, Oliver Cromwell in 1658, monarchy was restored with the return of Charles II. He arrived in Dover from the continent, and then travelled on to London via Canterbury. Samuel Pepys who was with the King, wrote in his diary for May 25th 1660, that 'the shouting and joy expressed by all is past imagination' (Latham, 1987). Did the people of Ditton celebrate when they heard the news of the Restoration of the monarchy? We can be sure that Sir Oliver Boteler, the Lord of the Manor, would have encouraged it. A new bell made by William Hatch, bell founder of Ulcombe had been installed in the tower of St. Peter's in 1656. It is inscribed TM CW WH 1656 and it is still rung today, as it was when Thomas Miller, a tenant farmer of Ditton Court, was churchwarden.

An amorino (putto), a winged cherub, from the Brewer monument

Chapter 6

A Late Stuart and Georgian Village: 1660-1837

Churchwardens, constables and overseers
Make up the round of commons and of peers;
With learning just enough to sign a name,
And skill sufficient parish rates to frame.

The Parish : A Satire. John Clare, 1793- 1864

The Restoration of the Monarchy with the return of Charles II to the throne was followed two years later by the reinstatement of the Book of Common Prayer. The Act of Uniformity decreed that all services from August 1662 would be from this book alone. During the Commonwealth the *Directory of Public Worship* had been introduced in 1645, but now many clergymen who did not conform to the Book of Common Prayer were expelled. One of these was Samuel French the vicar of West Malling. It is possible that Theophilus Jackson, rector of Ditton was also ejected at this time as a new appointment to St Peter's Church was made in 1663. This was the Reverend William Jole, who noted at the commencement of the book of register of births, marriages and burials *Inducted Rector of Ditton Anno Dom 1st August 1663.*

William Jole was to be one of the last resident rectors for about a hundred and eighty years, and perhaps the last for almost two hundred years to have his own children baptised in this parish church. With the existence of church registers from 1663 as well as memorial stones, we are able to build up a picture of William Jole and his family. He would have lived in the rectory in Kiln Barn Road, which is described in a later glebe terrier as *a manse or Rectory including ye parsonage House, Barn Yard and gardens, measuring by estimation about 1 acre.* We know that the house was thatched and had its own well, but when William Jole arrived the rectory was in a very poor condition. The Archdeacon of Rochester's Visitation in 1663 reported that 'the parsonage house being totally in decay and also the fences about the same' (Warner, 1994). Around the parish the rector had his own farm (glebe) land, 3 acres of woodland, half an acre of land behind what is now Stream Cottage, 3 acres of arable or hop land now in the area of Primrose Drive and Nursery Road, and one piece of arable of 3 acres near Mill Hall. We know from a later document of the 1680s that this was in a field called Mil-hale Field and described as 'bounded out with 3 stones pitched in the ground'. It was very common at that time for the parson to spend much time in farming, as described by Henry Fielding in *Joseph Andrews* of Parson Trulliber, who 'was a parson on Sundays, but all the other six might properly be called a farmer'. Financially he would have been largely supported by tithe from the produce of the land as well as from a tithe on woodland. This was by no means always the case in Kent, and a note in the church register for 1711 states: 'Memorandum that every acre of woodland in the parish of Ditton by immemorial custom pays tythe to the Rector'. In May 1665 he married Katherine Adye of West Malling in Aylesford Church, and then according to the new register, their firstborn son, Daniel, was baptised on March 8th, 1665. The confusion of a child appearing to be baptised before his parents were married, is due to the fact that until the calendar change in 1752, the new year commenced on March 25th, thus May would be before March! As the Book of Common Prayer declared at that time 'The year of our LORD in the Church of ENGLAND beginneth the Twenty Fifth Day of March'. Further children followed: Anne in 1670, Thomas in 1672, William in 1675 and Mary in 1676. William junior died in 1675 and is commemorated in a small floor monument by the south of the chancel arch, Katherine died in 1677 after only 12 years of married life (she is commemorated in memorial stone in the sanctuary of the chancel) and William Jole died the following year .He is commemorated in the centre of the chancel as *Hic jacet Guiliemus Jole…ecclesiae rector…anno domini 1678.* We have a small glimpse of his personality in a margin note on a document 'The Rector Jole was a joli old soul'.

William Jole's successor as Rector, Joseph Smith, died within a year of his appointment and the Rev'd Thomas Tilson, who had been vicar of Aylesford since 1666, was given the additional appointment as rector of Ditton, a post he held until 1702. One distinguished person whose funeral Thomas Tilson carried out in 1685 was for 'Mr William Boghurst of London'. We do not know where the Boghurst family lived in Ditton, but another John and Henry were buried in 1692. William Boghust (of London) was a well known courageous apothecary at the time of the bubonic plague (The Great Plague) in 1665. He wrote an account of the plague entitled *Loimographia,* in which he graphically described how 'I rendered myself familiar with the disease and dressed forty sores in a day, held the pulse of patients in their beds, let blood, administered clysters, held them in their beds to keep from strangling and choking. Then if people had nobody to help them, I helped to lay them forth out of bed, into the coffin and accompanied them to the ground' (Defoe, 1962). Such would have been the risk to his own life, that Samuel Pepys wrote that by October 1665, there was only one apothecary still alive in Westminster.

At the Restoration in 1660 the major land owners in the parish of Ditton continued to be the Boteler family of Barham Court of Teston for Ditton Court, and the Brewer family for Ditton Place. We can obtain an indication of the number of houses in the parish and of their size in the Hearth Tax assessment made in 1664 (Harrington, Pearson and Rose, 2000). This tax was the major source of government revenue, and was collected twice a year from 1662 to 1689 when it was replaced by the Window Tax. A 'Chimney Tax', as it was often called was payable at two shilling for each chimney, each year. Exemptions were made if the property was of particularly low value. In Ditton in 1664 there were only 20 properties, only one of which was 'not chargeable'. By contrast East Malling had 111 houses, thirty of which did not pay. These figures reveal the differences in housing density between neighbouring parishes; Ditton's ratio was about 50 acres per house and East Malling's, 25. In contrast to all the neighbouring villages, Ditton had the fewest non-payers. With only one out of 20, this contrasted with the overall Kentish average of just over 30% of properties. In Ditton the largest house, Ditton Place paid for nine hearths, while Ditton Court, Stream Cottage (then one house) and 'the Parsonage House' paid for five each. Four other fairly large houses in the parish with four to seven hearths cannot be specifically identified, but would have been Borough Court, Church Mill House, Ditton Farm (Cobdown Farmhouse) and Mill Hall Mill House. Altogether these figures suggest that Ditton was a sparsely populated parish, but a relatively prosperous community without a great gulf between the size of houses of the rich and poor. Even the largest house, Ditton Place, was modest in size in comparison with the houses of other parish landowners such as Boteler at Barham Court (18 hearths), Twisden at Bradbourne (23), and Colepepper at Preston Hall (27), but even these look modest in comparison with the Duke of Dorset's Knole Park, Sevenoaks with its 85 hearths!

The names of all the occupiers are given in the Hearth Tax assessments, such as 'Jesper Boreman five hearths'. From other records we know that the Boreman family had lived in Stream Cottage, then as one house, for nearly a hundred years. The family occupation had evolved from farming to tanning during the 17th century, and what had been a traditional 'Wealden Hall House' with a central two storied open hall with central hearth, by now had five fireplaces and an upper floor in the hall. The raw materials for tanning: animal hides, oak bark from Oaken Wood, lime from the kiln at Kiln Barn, and plenty of water were freely available, and this and another tannery across the stream from Church Mill

A Tudor fireplace in Stream Cottage. One of the five hearths in this house paid for by Jesper Boreman in 1664

House operated late into the 18th century. Adjacent to these houses must have been water filled pits where the leather was exposed to lime, then for months to increasing concentrations of tannin from the oak bark. Jesper Boreman must have made a good living from his trade, for when he died in 1688 a 'True and perfect Inventory of all and singillar Goods and Chattles of Jesper Borman late of Ditton in the County of Kent Tanner' was made with items listed for each room showing a very good standard of living (the original spelling has been retained) (Davidson, J. 2005)

In the Kitchin and Buttery
One table and form. One settle two wooden chairs one chair table; one other settle; one cupboard, one other cupboard. Three joyne stooles. Two pair of andirons, three pair of pothangers. Five Spitts, two iron dripping pans, one gridiron, one jack, one iron back. One drop oven door, one iron peel, one pair of tongs, one fendor.
Pewter and Brass, thirteen bowles, six drink vesells two olde tables and some other small things.

In the Brewhouse
One olde furnace and seven tubs and keelers, two pails.

In the Chamber over the Kitchin

One Bedsteade curtains and valons. Two feather beds, two feather bolsters. Two pillows. One Rugg and blankets, five leather chairs, one table and five joyne stools. One sideboard cupboard. Two pairs andirons. One fine shovel two pairs of tonges.

In the Buttery Chamber

Three bedsteads three flock beds and althings theretoo belonging. Four Chests and one box. One joyne stoole. Eleven pair of sheets, Two dozen and a half of napkins. Half a dozen of table cloths and towels.

In the Brewhouse Chamber

One old bedsteddle , one chest and one trunk.

Without Doors

Wood in the yard and one Cow and one Hogg . For Lumbar and things not seen and forgotten.

The total value of these goods together with 'his purse and wearing apparel' came to £29.17.6d. Of particular importance to Jesper Borman was the quality of his bedding. This was often the most luxurious feature in the houses of the middle classes. The major bed with curtains was obviously a four poster, and had plenty of comfort with feather bed and bolsters. By contrast the inventory of a cottage agricultural labourer included: 'One bellows, one tongs, one joint stool, one iron pot, three pewter dishes, four plates, three earthen pans, one bedstead and bedding'.

In an altogether different economic bracket was Judge Sir Thomas Twisden (1602-1682) who bought Bradbourne House in East Malling in the 1650s (Twisden, 1939: Hatton and Hatton, 1945). He was a lawyer by profession, and as a judge was involved in the sentencing of John Bunyan and the Quaker George Fox, both prominent non-conformists. He was also an M.P. for Maidstone, and after being knighted in 1660 was given a baronetcy in 1666. Sir Thomas desired to turn Bradbourne into an estate worthy of his status, and purchased much

Sir Thomas Twisden, 1601-1682,
the first Baronet of Bradbourne

land in East Malling and Ditton, including Borough Court, Ditton Farm, (Cobdown) and Mill Hall Mill and farm. Just before his death, his son Roger (the eventual second baronet) negotiated successfully in 1676 to move the road that ran from East Malling to Larkfield away from Bradbourne House, thus improving the layout of his park and increasing his privacy (Melling, 1959). This became 'New Road' and had the effect of removing a crossroads from the centre of Larkfield. The Bradbourne Park then extended from Larkfield to East Malling Church and approximately from the border of Ditton in the east to Winterfield Lane (later Clare Park) in the west. A ha ha was made across the New Road, creating the impression of an uninterrupted avenue of trees. Part of the later park wall still exists, running on the Ditton parish border by a section of the footpath from Ditton Green to East Malling. In the 1680s, the second baronet Sir Roger Twisden commissioned Abraham Walter, a tenant farmer of Larkfield and an efficient cartographer, to draw a series of maps of his estate. These most informative coloured maps cover among other areas Bradbourne Park, Court Lodge Farm East Malling, Larkfield Farm, Gig Hill Farm, Lunsford, and Broadwater Farm together with 'A true Map of Brook Court Farm (alias) Burrough Court Farm in the Parish of Ditton in the County of Kent and A Mapp of a farm in the Parish of Ditton in Kent in the occupation of John Tomlin'. They provide a remarkably detailed record of the whole estate, and are the earliest maps in existence of any part of Ditton. The maps have symbolic sketches of each farmhouse and mill, and they give field names with acreage and some indications of land use, as well as of the number and variety of trees growing in hedgerows and fields. They give a good picture of farming in Ditton at the end of the 17th century.

The original house and farm of Borough Court purchased from the Shakerley family was about 40 acres in extent. Thomas Twisden was able to purchase further land almost doubling the size of the farm, and also linking it directly to the River Medway. Perhaps the Shakerley family produced some hops for their own brewing as one small field was called 'Old Hop Ground'. By the 1680s this field, together with three others near to the farmhouse were identified as 'mowing land', vital for hay fodder for animal production and motive power. A magnificent new stable block had just been completed at Bradbourne House which could have relied upon hay from these productive meadows. Adjacent to the farmhouse was an orchard, and within a short distance, a small shaw (wood), ideal for fuel and fencing. Being a mixed farm, some fields such as 'The Rushes' and 'The Alders' would be used for grazing, while various cereals such as wheat, oats and barley would have been the major crops of the arable fields. A later map of Borough Court Farm from the 1770s, shows that in the intervening years from the 1680s, a number of the small fields had been linked together into larger units. This is generally associated with a desire for increased efficiency and productivity.

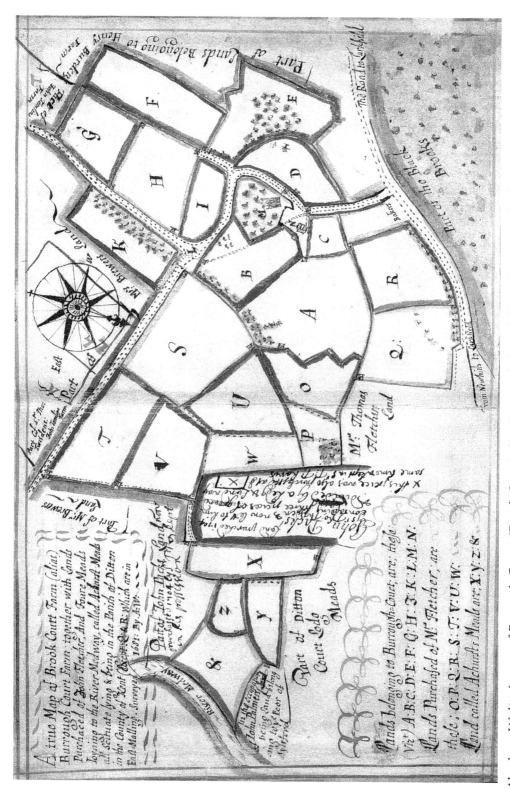

Abraham Walter's map of Borough Court (Brook Court alias Burrough Court) Farm in 1681. The farmhouse is located in field M.

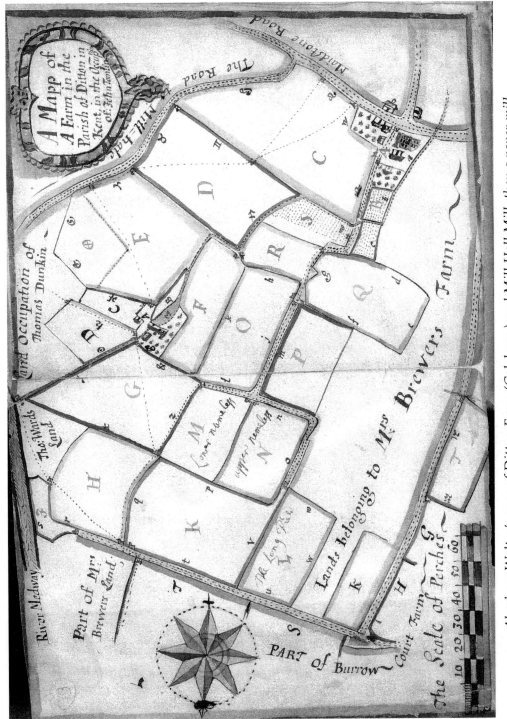

Abraham Walter's map of Ditton Farm (Cobdown) and Mill Hall Mill, then a paper mill.

Cobdown Farmhouse in 2011. The village stocks were located outside this house.

Ditton Farm (Cobdown Farm), farmed by John Tomlin, was a substantial holding of 122 acres of arable and pasture. Being on slightly higher ground further from the river levels it had only two acres of meadow land for hay, one acre of which is confusingly entitled 'The two hop spots'. Another field near the farm yard was called 'Hopgarden field'. In the centre of the farmland was the sandy outcrop of 'Copdowne', ideal for the grazing of sheep. The farmhouse, then with two small orchards and a number of nearby barns and stables, still remains to this day. Part of this farm estate included Mill Hall Mill. This was a separate small holding of about six acres. Prior to the 1680s the function of this mill had changed from corn grinding to paper making and a four acre field to the west of the mill was called 'Papermill Field'. Papermaking was becoming an important industry in mid-Kent following the initial conversion of a corn mill to a paper mill at Dartford by John Spilman in 1588 (Hills, 1988). Prior to this time much paper was imported from the continent. Kent was now well placed to supply this need, with easy access to and from London where a good source of rags was available, and on streams such as the Ditton Stream, and at Maidstone the River Len and Loose Stream, pure, iron free water was available for power as well as for the processes of manufacture. Power from the water wheel was now utilised to beat rags into a pulp prior to their being spread on the frame of the paper mould. This mill continued to manufacture paper until about 1830 when it was reconverted to flour production and eventually demolished in the mid 1940s (Fuller, 1980).

The map maker Abraham Walter made a particular point of identifying the trees growing on the land of Ditton Farm. He noted on the edge of a table 'Upon this farm be all sorts of trees'. By using alphabetical identification symbols, he located over 370 oak, ash and elm trees. Each tree type was sub-classified as follows:

Timber oaks 59: Young oaks 24: Pollard oaks 10.
Timber elm 238: Young elms 92: Pollard elm 113.
Spire ashes 17:   Poll ashes 16: Young ashes 15.

This highlights the importance of trees and their continual regeneration in the rural economy. These hardwood trees were important for buildings, furniture, tools, farm and domestic implements as well as a potential source of fuel.

Until the coming of the M 20 motorway bypassing Ditton in 1971, the A20, London Road passing Wrotham Heath and on to Maidstone was the major route from London to Ashford, Hythe and Folkestone. This first detailed road survey of England by John Ogilby, 'Cosmographer to His Majesty' (Ogilby, 1675) was presented as a series of strip maps. Although Ditton figures on the road from 'London to Hith' (Hythe), it is surprisingly not on the main route from London to Maidstone. From London the Hythe road went in two possible directions from Kingsdown on the North Downs, one on to Stansted (*Stanstead*) then to Trottiscliffe (*Croseley*) and on to Addington, joining the present A 20 at the Offham turn. This road then proceeded to Ditton Corner, where it made a sharp turn to Aylesford (*Aylisford*), (probably the origin of the name Ditton Corner), bypassing Maidstone near Penenden Heath and on to Bearsted (*Barsted*). The alternative road from Kingsdown dropped down the North Downs to Wrotham (*Rotham),* on to Offham (*Offam*) then an extensive wooded traverse through what became Malling aerodrome (Kings Hill) and on the ridge apex through Oaken Wood, just across the border from Ditton in the parish of Barming, and down into Maidstone across *a stone bridge.* This was the main route from London to Maidstone, and rejoined the more northerly route at Penenden Heath (*Pickendon Heath),* and then on to Hythe. A confirmation of the importance of this more southerly woodland traverse as the major route from London is provided by a map of The Manor of East Malling surveyed in 1706. The road through Ditton from Larkfield is given no particular priority, but the more southerly road through Oaken Wood is described in large letters as **LONDON ROAD.** The status of the present A20, which Hasted described in 1798 as *the high road from London, through Wrotham, to Maidstone,* changed with the turnpiking of this part of the road in around 1760.

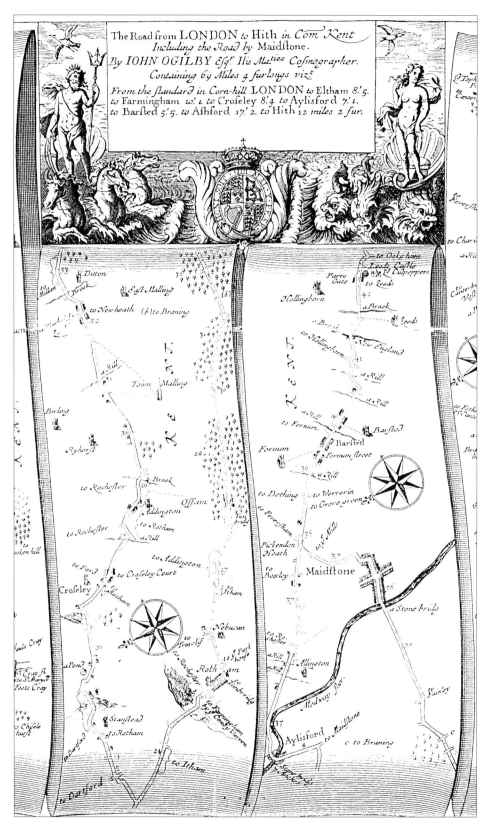

Part of the London to Hith (Hythe) Road from Britannia, a Description of Principal Roads thereof *by John Ogilby, 1675*

From 1555 all roads had become the responsibility of each parish to repair and maintain, but the tremendous variability in standard was most frustrating for travellers. Turnpikes were first introduced into England as privately financed toll roads in 1663 of a more uniform and higher standard. The southern section of the old Hythe road from Wrotham Heath via Offham was turnpiked as far as the North Pole Inn, and then down the hill to Teston in 1773. Much of the remainder of this once important route became what is now the narrow wooded North Pole Road to Barming Heath!

A consequence of the turnpiking of the road through Ditton was that the parish was no longer responsible for the maintenance of this parish road. However, it was obliged to pay a sum of money from the parish rates, called Composition, directly to the turnpike trust. In 1772 this is described as 'Paid the Composition to the Highways and in the following year Paid to the Turnpike Road'. The turnpike trust collected money from travellers at each turnpike gate with a published scale of charges such as 'for every horse, mule, ass or other beast laden or unladen the sum of twopence'. There were always a number of exemptions: 'persons going to their usual place of worship; conveying the mails; conveying arms or baggage of soldiers; prisoners sent by legal warrant'. The nearest gate to Ditton was at Larkfield on the north side of the road by the Hundred Court House. The single storied toll-house was demolished in the 1960s. In addition to turnpike gates, familiar features for travellers along most major roads were inns and public houses. Accommodation could be demanded at inns whereas public houses were solely for the consumption of alcoholic drinks. There was a public house in Ditton for much of the 18th century and early 19th century on the London Road near the present entrance to Ditton Place and Streamside. It had been built in 1713, when it was described as a 'New House and malt House'. From the 1730s to 1760s it was owned by Thomas Comber, who in addition to brewing and selling beer had a small farm. In the mid 19th century a new public house, The Walnut Tree, was built in Bradbourne Lane. The former public house became a private house, Ivy House, and was demolished in the 1920s during road widening. Ale houses at that time were of very variable quality as described by Lord Torrington in September 1790. He would have travelled from London passing through Ditton and turned toward Aylesford. 'We enter'd Aylesford by a steep old stone bridge: and so to the Anchor Ale House, as bad a stop as could be, with most miserable stabling. Our landlord was a surly ignorant Brute'. (Andrews, 1954). Things were rather different in 1873 when Benjamin Harrison, the archaeologist and shopkeeper from Ightham, visited Aylesford. 'In the inn by the bridge at Aylesford, we had the best bread and cheese in the cleanest inn I ever saw.' (Harrison, 1928).

Ogilby's description *a Brook* where the London to Hythe road crossed the Ditton

A turnpike milestone on the London Road, Ditton, in 2011

stream is an indication that there was a bridge here. He used the term *a Rill* when there was a ford as of the stream from *Town Malling* to Leybourne. Before the publication of Ogilby's road atlas there were two lengths of English mile! The Long Mile of 2,428 yards was the most commonly used, but following Ogilby's use, the 'Statute Mile' of 1,760 yards became standard. His atlas showed that Ditton was 33 miles from London, a little longer than the later direct route over Wrotham Hill described by Hasted in 1798 as 'at the thirty-first milestone'. Milestones were not widely used until they were made obligatory for all turnpike roads in1766. One reason for the standardisation of road mileage was to unify charges for mail which were then based on the number of miles conveyed. The route for mail from London to this part of central Kent was not via the direct route from London. Since 1660 there were two major mail routes through the county: the North Kent, Watling Street route to Rochester, Canterbury and Dover, and the more southerly route to Rye via Sevenoaks and Tonbridge. Mail for the central part of Kent came from Rochester to Maidstone and then to this locality there were deliveries to West Malling via Larkfield on three days of the week.

We can obtain a clear picture of the social and caring side of the community of Ditton in the 18th century from the work of the Overseer of the Poor as recorded in the account book from 1731. There were probably no more than about twenty households in the parish including those associated with two mills (one paper making), one or two tanneries, four farms, one or two smallholdings (one linked to the public house), and one 'gentleman's residence', Ditton Place. The Overseer was appointed annually by a meeting of the chief inhabitants, the Vestry, from among the farmers, millers etc. and this task rotated every few years among them. They collected an annual Poor Rate from all landowners according to their area of land. In the earlier years of the century a rate of one shilling or one shilling and sixpence in the pound was quite adequate, but in the 1790s, with poor harvests and increasing hardships caused by the Napoleonic Wars, the rate was increased to five shillings in the pound. Each year the accounts had to be ratified and signed by a local magistrate such as Sir Roger Twisden of Bradbourne, or Sir Robert Style of Wateringbury Place.

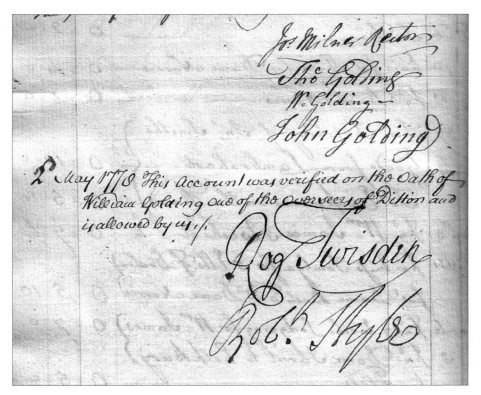

The accounts of William Golding, Overseer of the Poor in 1777, and ratified by other members of the vestry, and two local magistrates, Sir Roger Twisden (the sixth Baronet) and Sir Robert Style.

One has the impression of a generally caring and kindly community, not only for the needy inhabitants, but also for many who were travelling on the London Road. One of the most regular payments was to widows with children. A widow Norris received a weekly payment of two shillings a week (the average wage at that time was six shillings) for over 25 years. Her rent and tithe were also paid, and in 1732 she was given a cow and a load of wood. In 1734 she was given a blanket and rug, three pairs of shoes for her children, a neck of mutton and a pint of wine! She was provided with nursing by Goody Atkins when she was ill. Later in 1747, her son John was given money for rent, but in 1752 coffins were provided for his three children. His widow was still receiving a weekly allowance in 1794. In addition to nursing, a doctor's fees would be paid, or transport to hospital. During a smallpox outbreak in 1739 payment was provided for nursing 'Widow King's girl' in East Malling. Clothes and shoes were frequently provided, or material to make shirts, shifts, breeches and bedding. Bastardy was a real economic problem for the Overseer in some communities as the mother and child (children) were supported from the parish budget. Legislation in 1744 made it mandatory for the mother to 'declare the father'. In Ditton in 1741 the Overseer paid 'for a licence and marrying of Margaret Evenden for swearing ye child'. National legislation in 1723 had encouraged parishes to set up a Poor House for the homeless and needy. The Ditton Vestry rented a cottage on The Green in 1760 for use as a Poor House, which was used until the establishment of the union Workhouse at King Hill, West Malling in 1834. The cottage was demolished when the first school building was erected in 1853.

In the days before media and mass literacy, news of national and international events might be obtained from travellers moving from London to the coast. For bona fide travellers such as military personnel and others who had a permit to move back to their rightful place of residence, a Pass could be obtained. This was a legal document obtained from a magistrate entitling the bearer to travel across country and to obtain a small some of money from a parish official. This was usually a churchwarden, and in 1679 the Ditton wardens gave sixpence *to* 'Thomas William a soldier belonging to the Duke of Monmouth'. At this time Monmouth was a popular commander of English Land Forces prior to his fateful battle of Sedgemoor in 1685. During the Napoleonic War sixpence was given 'to a crippled soldier with a pass' in 1812. Earlier in the war they relieved 'three soldiers wives with a pass'. There were many others who were helped on their way just because they were in need: 1750, 'gave a poor man on the road; 1765 Gave to four poor peepel; 1776 carried a woman in distress to Maidstone'; 1799, 'gave to a wounded soldier'. On occasions when a traveller died on the road or in 1742 when 'a poor woman who Dy'd in hopping at Mr. Golding's', they were given burial at the expense of the parish. On another occasion when in1768 'a woman was taken ill on ye road and could not go no further', she was given nursing for 14 weeks which cost the parish almost £5 out of an annual budget of £29.

For needy people within a community, their plight could be discussed with the Overseer of the Poor who, with a churchwarden, might be available in the church on one Sunday afternoon each month. If you were unhappy about the decision of the officers, you could appeal to a local magistrate for a review of the case. The officers of the parish vestry also included the Surveyor of Highways (waywarden) and constable (borsholder) who would also meet in the church vestry under the usual chairmanship of the rector. The waywarden organised road maintenance, and in addition to Statute Labour (see previous chapter) could employ able bodied poor. The Poor accounts have numerous references to the purchase of stone from the various small quarries, and in 1746 Mr Seager (a tanner), was paid as 'the Surveyor of Highways for stones and beer'. Beer was the frequent reward for the hard work of road repair. A quarry which could have supplied stone was one on the The Green by the church. A drawing by J. C. Nattes in 1816 shows two men working in this quarry with a pick and shovel. As Ditton was a small parish, an agreement was made with Aylesford in 1759 that 'Ditton and Myl halle have the same borsholder, who by custom should be chosen alternately from each'. One constable in the middle of the 18th century was a William Goodhew. On occasions he was given expenses for carrying out an arrest warrant and taking the accused to a magistrate. In the early years of the Napoleonic War in 1795 he compiled a list of those who could serve in the militia. Perhaps his popularity had improved in the parish by this time as a few years earlier a pencil note on the Overseer's accounts declared 'Goodhew is an old fool and be dam'd to him!'. Later in 1812 the churchwardens' accounts record 'Paid Borsholder and Men for padrolling the parish in the night'. If needed, there were stocks on the side of the London Road near Ditton (Cobdown) Farm referred to in 1759: 'Ditton usually has had stocks of its own in the street near Sir Roger Twisden's farm house now occupied by John Sidgier'. These were usually used for a three hour period of public humiliation for being drunk and disorderly, and right opposite the public house! At this time there were still many capital offences, although transportation to America began in 1718 and to Australia in 1790. This was an ever present threat for many misdemeanours, such as happened to Elizabeth Weller of East Malling in 1815, who was transported for seven years for stealing linen and apparel worth 10 pence (Melling, 1969).

Digging stone in Ditton Quarry on The Green. A drawing by J. C. Nattes, July 1816

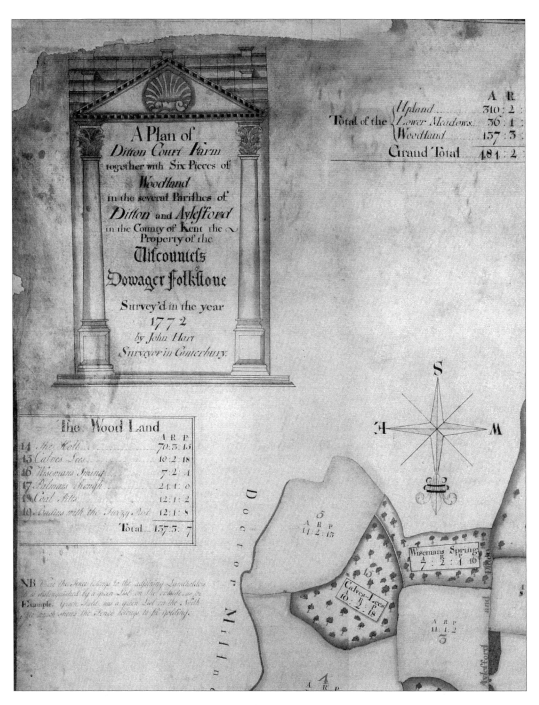

A Plan of
Ditton Court Farm
together with Six Pieces of
Woodland
in the several Parishes of
Ditton and Aylesford
in the County of Kent the
Property of the
Viscountess
Dowager Folkstone

Survey'd in the year
1772
by John Hart
Surveyor in Canterbury.

Total of the		A	R	
	Upland	310	2	
	Lower Meadows	36	1	
	Woodland	157	3	
Grand Total		484	2	

The Wood Land		A	R	P
14	The Holt	70	3	15
15	Calves Lees	10	2	18
16	Wisemans Spring	7	2	4
17	Palmers Slaugh	24	1	0
18	Coal Pits	12	1	2
19	Coaling with the Furzy Post	12	1	8
	Total	157	3	7

NB Were the Fence belongs to the adjoining Landholders
is distinguished by a green Line on the outside, as for
Example, Green Field, has a green Line on the North
side, which shews the Fence belongs to the holding.

A description of maps drawn in 1772

The Dowager Countess Folkestone, painted by Thomas Gainsborough in 1778

Throughout the 18th century the ownership of much of Ditton continued to be in the hands of three families of non-residents (sometimes called in the churchwardens' account book, 'Forringers'): Sir Philip Boteler of Barham Court, Sir Roger Twisden of Bradbourne and Sir Thomas Colepeper of Preston Hall. These and others would fit Daniel Defoe's description of the Maidstone area in the 1720s: 'The country everywhere spangled with populous villages, and delicious seats of the nobility and gentry...a very agreeable place to live in.' (Defoe,1986). With all three of these families, however, the maintenance of a male line of succession carrying the family estate and name was to be a major problem and ownership of land followed a pattern of tortuous complexity!

Sir Philip Boteler, Lord of the Manor of Ditton who died in 1772, had no heirs and his Barham Court estate was divided into three parts for members of the Bouverie family from which his grandmother, Anne, was a member. The Manor of Ditton, including Ditton Court Farm was the portion of the estate allocated to Elizabeth, the Dowager Viscountess of Folkestone. She immediately commissioned a cartographer J. Hunt from Canterbury to draw detailed maps of this part of her estate. These beautifully drawn maps show farm buildings, fields with name and area in acres, and woodland.

When Sir Thomas Colepeper of Preston Hall died in 1723, his heir was his sister Alicia, who was married four times. Her second marriage to Sir Thomas Taylor in 1692, and her fourth to Dr John Milner in 1723, took place in St.Peter's Church, Ditton. This fourth husband died in 1724, and having outlived four

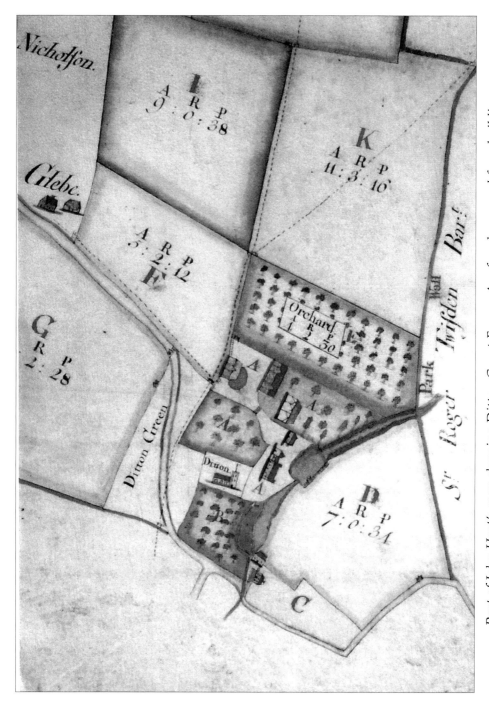

Part of John Hart's map showing Ditton Court Farm. A = farmhouse and farm buildings.
C = Church Mill and mill house. The Rectory in Kiln Barn Road is Glebe.

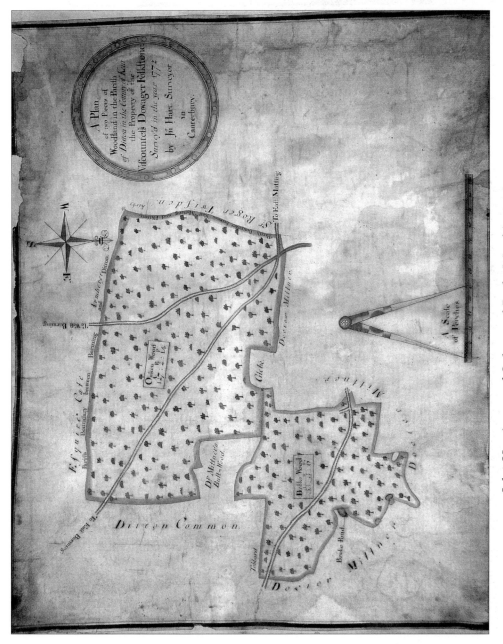

John Hart's map of Oaken and Broke Wood in 1772

83

husbands and a number of children, she died in 1734 aged 77. Curiously, the Ditton overseers account book still called her 'The Lady Taylor' until her death. Thus with the end of the line of Colepeper ownership that extended back to the 13th century, the Preston Hall Estate, including parts of Ditton, passed to her last husband's brother, Dr Charles Milner. He lived at Preston Hall until his death in 1771, leaving this estate to a nephew, the Rev'd Joseph Butler who was rector of Ditton and Burham. A condition of inheritance was that he changed his name to Milner and he is then described in the church account book as 'The Rev: Doc. Milnor'. He died childless in 1784, and after the death of his widow Sarah in 1803, the estate was inherited by a nephew Charles Cotton also on condition that he changed his name to Milner. He was succeeded by his son Charles in 1836, who enlarged the estate by purchasing the Manor of Ditton, including Ditton Court and a major part of Oaken Wood, from Viscountess Folkestone's grandson, Philip Pusey in 1840. Thus ended a 220 year family link with the Manor of Ditton. Charles Milner then owned well over 650 acres of a parish of 1073 acres. However he died four years later, and his younger brother Colonel Henry Milner sold the whole Preston Hall estate to Edward Ladd Betts in 1848.

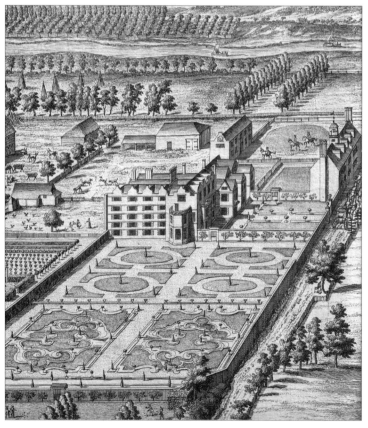

Preston Hall in the time of Sir Thomas Colepeper, drawn by J. Kip. It was described in 1790 by Lord Torrington as 'a pleasant green place in a delicious country.' (Andrews, 1954). This house was demolished in 1850.

The other major 'foreign' landowner in Ditton in the 18th century was the Twisden family. Their house, Bradbourne, was a third of a mile over the Ditton border! Their portion of the parish which included Borough Court Farm, Ditton Farm, and Mill Hall Mill, nearly two hundred acres in all, had been purchased by Sir Thomas Twisden, and passed to his son Sir Roger Twisden in 1682. When he died in 1702 his son, also Roger, became the third baronet, and with his wife Anne he instigated a rebuilding of the west front of the house between 1712 and 1715. This part of the house is renowned for its outstanding brickwork. Later in the century the sixth baronet, Sir Roger Twisden (1737-1779) made additions to the southern side of the house in the Adam style and linked this to major landscape changes with the formation of a long serpentine lake and island. He died before his only child Rebecca was born, and because his father had disinherited his brother William for a supposedly unsuitable marriage, the estates and title of the baronetcy passed to his youngest brother, John Papillon Twisden. John had to sell parts of the estate, including the portion on the other side of New Road, East Malling, which eventually became Clare Park. Rebecca married Thomas Law Hodges, M.P. from Benenden in 1802 and eventually, after much wrangling, inherited the major part of the Twisden estate, including the two Ditton farms and mill, and the park of Bradbourne House. The mansion house was retained by a cousin, Captain John Twisden. Much of the park was converted to agricultural use and became the basis of Park Farm, Bradbourne, on the western border of Ditton.

Bradbourne House drawn by R. Godfrey about 1780

The purchase of Ditton Place by Thomas Golding from the long established Brewer family around 1700 marked the beginning of a family association with the parish which would last a hundred and fifty years. Towards the end of the 18th century various members of the family would not only be residents of the farm estate of Ditton Place, but tenants of Ditton Court Farm as well as of Mill Hall paper mill. Like the Brewers before them, they left conspicuous reminders of their presence in the form of a number of hanging memorials with a family coat of arms in St Peter's Church, some large table tombs, as well as a family vault in the churchyard. Perhaps the family's most lasting memorial is in the development of the well-known hop variety Golding. According to a later Rector of Ditton, John Stratton, who wrote about hops and hop pickers, 'the Golding, [was] originally grown at Ditton Place, and called after the name of the then owner'. A legacy of greater benefit to the poor of Ditton was a bequest by Thomas Golding in 1705 to provide five shillings' worth of bread on Christmas and Easter days.

John Golding (1727-1807) moved into Ditton Place in 1770, the year before his marriage to Ann Stimpson in1771. Like the other farmers, millers and tanners of the parish oligarchy, he took his turn as churchwarden and overseer of the poor, keeping the accounts in an immaculate copperplate handwriting. As with many families of the period, he and his wife outlived their children, Oliver, William and Mary Ann, the youngest daughter. All are commemorated in St Peter's Church. Perhaps there was a particular affection for Mary Ann who died at the age of 23 in 1805 as she is remembered on three monuments. When John Golding died in 1807, Ditton Place passed to his eldest son Thomas. Thomas might well have been a competent musician as he had a chamber organ at Ditton Place which he had purchased from Bartholomew Davis a former organist of West Malling. Thomas died in 1818 at the age of 46, and Ditton Place passed to a younger brother John. He lovingly remembered him with a monument in St Peter's Church: 'This monument is erected by his affectionate brother, John Golding, Esq., of Ditton Place'.

The Golding family coat of arms on a hanging monument in St Peter's Church

Financial support for the church was by a compulsory Church Rate. This was eventually abolished in 1868. In an era before the existence of a *Treasurer*, the churchwardens worked out an assessment based on the size of property, and kept a book of accounts. These exist from 1677 and each year begins with this example statement: 'An assessment made ye 20 day of September toward repair of ye said Parish Church at ninepence in the pound as followeth from Easter 1769 to Easter 1770.' There then follows a list of landowners/tenants, and the amount they paid in the year.

		£	s	d
George Luck	(Ditton Court Farm)	2	9	6
John Golding	(Ditton Place)	1	17	6
John Sidgier	(Ditton Farm)		18	9
Thomas Golding	(Paper Mill, Mill Hall Mill)		17	3
William Goodhew	(Tan Yard)		4	6
Jane Luck	(Flour Mill, Church Mill)		8	7
William Golding			2	7

Out dwellers

		£	s	d
The Earl of Aylesford	(The Friars, Aylesford)		1	6
Sir Philip Boteler	(Barham Court, Teston)	1	2	6
Sir Roger Twisden	(Bradbourne House, East Malling)	1	7	9
Mr Milner	(Preston Hall, Aylesford)		10	6
Edward Brown late Seager	(Owner of a tanyard)		13	6
Edward Brown late Comber	(Owner of the Public House)		9	9

Etc.

In this particular year the Church Rate raised £12 and £12.14.8d was spent. There were few major changes in the appearance of St Peter's Church between the Restoration and the mid-19th century, and over the years there were steady payments for repair and maintenance, such as for 3,030 shingles in 1687 and 6,000 tiles in 1773 and a new weather vane in 1814. The sundial which stood in the churchyard was repaired in 1759 and 1782, and in 1831 a new one purchased. One can imagine that all windows were of clear glass, the walls were whitewashed, and the nave was filled with 12 box pews allocated to the major houses in the parish, with a few smaller ones for two or three people and some benches for the poor. In 1759 there were only 75 people living in the parish in 15 families! The Creed and Lord's Prayer were on painted boards at the east end of the chancel which had been put there in 1663. There was a three-decker pulpit at the north front of the nave which had been constructed by a local carpenter in 1670, with a top deck for preaching, a middle deck for the parson to lead the service and the bottom deck for the parish clerk. The pulpit had a 'cushion of crimson velvet' on which the Bible was placed. The Bible was: 'a large folio Bible of the last translation, printed by Robert Barker 1613'. This was only the second printing of the new King James Bible, by the King's printer. In 1670 the church had been told that 'the clerk to have a seat under the minister's reading pew, to rail the communion table as formerly and to provide a new cover for the font'. In 1759 the table was described as 'a decent communion table', but 'there was no proper carpet to cover ye communion table in time of Divine Service'. Eventually in 1829 the church purchased 'A new blue cloth for the Communion table ordered by the Archdeacon'. A major addition to the seating accommodation took place in 1790 with the erection of the gallery. This was constructed by Mr G. Hunt of Aylesford at a cost of £21 and paid for by public subscription. Half of this amount was paid by John Golding of Ditton Place. The regular services of Morning and Evening Prayer would have taken place each Sunday, with Evening Prayer being in the afternoon in the winter. Payments for 'Bread and Wine four times' in 1759, show how infrequently Holy Communion was celebrated each year, which was quite normal throughout England until the middle of the 19th century. Throughout the 18th century there was often little singing in most village churches. Sometimes a few men would sing a metrical psalm, and after 1770 instruments such as flutes and violins might act as an accompaniment.

The organ built by Argent of Colchester and used in St Peter's Church from 1814 to 1959. It was sold to the church by Thomas Golding of Ditton Place.

Organs were almost exclusively found in town churches at this time, such as locally at West Malling and All Saints, Maidstone. We have no evidence of instruments in Ditton Church before 1814. In 1805 the church purchased a pitch pipe for the leading singer, usually the parish clerk, to sound the right note. In 1814, Thomas Golding of Ditton Place sold his forty year-old organ to the church for £26. Like the gallery, this was paid for by public subscription, and the large additional sum for the organist fee paid from the church rates. In 1819 for example, the Church Rate raised £28 of which £15 was payment for the organist. This is exceptional for a very small country church at this time, and Ditton Church was about fifty years ahead of its other parish neighbours, most of whom had their first organs from the second half of the 19th century. The organ was placed in the gallery, and in 1819 the church purchased 'two dozen Psalm Books for the children and congregation'. When the church historian, Sir Stephen Glynne visited the church in the 1830s he noted: 'There is an organ played with the fingers.' (Glynne, 1877). This would be in contrast to barrel organs which were becoming popular at this time. This fine chamber organ built by Argent of Colchester in 1774 was sold to Rochester Cathedral in 1959, but now resides in Suffolk (Wilson, 1968).

One service that was always held during this period was 'A Form of prayer with Thanksgiving to be used yearly upon the fifth day of November'. The day must have been accompanied by much bell ringing year after year, as in 1763 when 'paid for ringing the Gunpowder Treason three shillings'. There were three bells but only two could be rung. An old one was described in 1759 as 'broke and has old characters round it', a second of 1656, and a third purchased in 1717 from a bell founder at Hunton for £7.8s. and inscribed **Edward Middleton C W 1717**. During the Napoleonic Wars there were payments for special forms of prayer in 1805: 'For a prayer for a General Thanksgiving for Nelsons's Victory'. In 1815: 'a form of prayer to be read in ye Church for a Victory gained of the French by Field Marshal Wellington [Waterloo]'.

Some payments in the churchwardens' account books refer to matters that we would define as secular, but at that time were expected duties. From Tudor times churchwardens had been pest control officers in each parish, and could pay small sums of money for dead vermin. There are numerous payments and some examples are found in 1683: 'three foxes and a polecat'; 1779: '2 hedgehogs, 76 sparrows'; 1811: 'Joseph Ralph 24 sparrows eggs and 12 sparrows'. In 1824 £1.6.11d was paid out for nearly four hundred sparrows. The boundaries of the parish had to be clearly identified and known by all, by walking around them.

Overleaf: Pages from the account book of John Golding, churchwarden, in 1834.
Page 90: Money raised by church rates; Page 91: Expenditure.

		£	s	d
1834	An Assessment made by John Golding and Thomas Allchin Church Wardens of the Parish of Ditton from Easter 1834 to Easter 1835 at Six Pence in the Pound Half Rents			
70..10..	John Golding Ditton Place his own	1	15	3
20.. ..	Thomas Allchin		10	
1.. ..	More Jos & Wm Golding's Plantation			6
110.. ..	Henry Ranger Court Lodge P. Pusey Esqr	2	15	
36..10	Richard Pemble Boro'Court Sir J. Twisden		18	3
	Out Dwellers			
90..	The Revd. Richd. Ward Rector	"	"	"
44..17.6	Chas. Miles Sir J. Twisden's Land	1	2	5½
93.. "	Philip Pusey Esqr. Woodland own	2	6	6
20.. ..	Chas. Milner Esqr &c Woodland own		10	
16.. ..	Chas. Milner Junr Floris Land		8	
4..15.	Thomas Spong own	2	4	½
3.. "	more Milner's Land	1		6
5..15..	more Sons of the Clergy	2	10	½
1.. 5..	Alfd. Wigan Esqr. own		7	½
..10..	Robert Tassell Sir John Twisden's Park			3
9..12.6	Thomas Andrews own Land	4		9¾
3..15..	John Hall Lord Aylesford's Land	1		10½
..5..	Thomas Browning own			1½
12.. ..	more Nicholson's Land		6	
5..10..	more Do Do	2		9
3.. 7.6	Ricd. & Jas. Upton Poor's Meads	1		8½
26.. ..	Stephen Spratt Flour Mill Sir J Twisden		13	
7..15..	Robt. Tassell Land Sir J Twisden	3		10
591..7.6		£	12.. 7.. 8½	
96 ---	deduct R. Revd A. Ward To cash in hand due		2.. 4.. 23	
495..17..6	to collect on from last years account		14..11..11	
		£		

1834	Disbursement of John Golding and Thomas Allchin Church Wardens of the Parish of Ditton from Easter 1834, to Easter 1835.	£	s	p
April 1	Pd. Smith Mat maker's Bill	1	6	3
11	Pd. Relph's Bill the Clerk for a half year	2	7	–
June 12	Pd. for Letter respecting Rochester Bridge			7½
	Pd. for 450 Sparrows at 1/4 each	9		6½
	Pd. for 2 Hedge Hogs - at 4d each			8
	Pd. for 24 Sparrows			6
July 23	The Bishop's Visitation at Tonbridge			
	Church Wardens — — £ 10 4			
	Incumbent — — 4 4			
	Curate — — 1 4	1	4	0
	Archdeacon's Procurations 5 6			
	Dean & Chapter's Pensions — 2 6			
	Paid the Bishop's Apparitor's Fees			
	Confirmation fees — 10 =			
	Citing Church Wardens to the Visitation 3 6			
	Do new Church Warden's Minister 5 =	1	1	0
	Attending the Visitation — 2 6			
	Paid the Incumbents Procurations		4	6
	Pd. Church Warden's expences attending the Visitation — —	1	2	10
July 28	Pd. for 40 Sparrows - at 1/4 each			10
Oct. 13	Pd. Relph the Clerk's half year's Bill	2	7	–
Nov 29	Pd. Thos Edmeads 57 Sparrows	1		2½
Decr 16	Pd. Spencer for 4 Pints of Sact Wine	8		
1835				
Mar 7	Pd. Terry's Bill repairs Church	12		
April 20	Pd. Richd Relph Clerk Half Year Bill	2	7	–
	By Balance due to the Parish	18	11	3¾
	£	14	11	11½

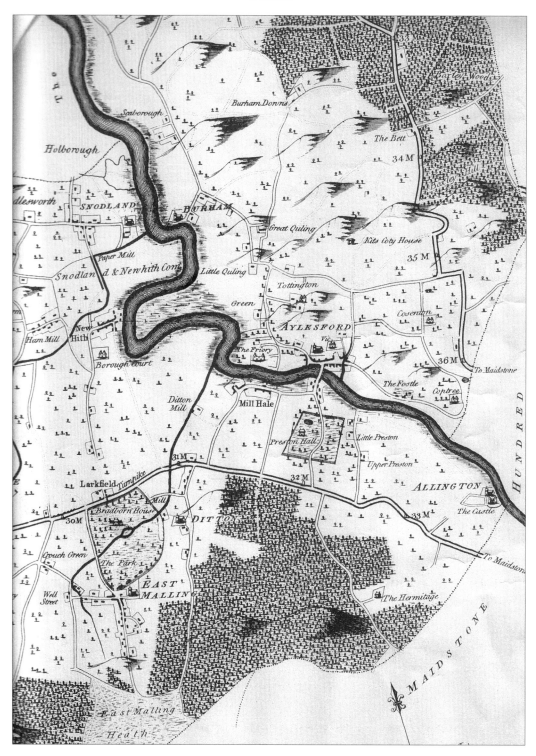

Map of the Hundred of Larkfield for Hasted'S History of Kent, surveyed in 1778

Payments were made for 'Going bounds' in 1770, 1789, 1792 and in 1834, when 'expenses going bounds' amounted to £5.19.4d out of and annual budget of £15. The expenses usually involved drink and cakes as subsistence for the eight or nine mile perambulation. The northern boundary of the parish was the River Medway, and in 1759 a boat was hired for this part 'for going by waters bound day two shillings'.

During the 18th century most of the rectors of Ditton held the living in plurality and did not live in the parish. Thomas Tilson (junior) followed his father as rector of Ditton and Aylesford in 1702, and remained rector until his death in 1750. He left a valuable bequest 'for the Poor of Ditton for ever the Interest of 100 pounds to be distributed annually in wheat and wood on All Saints Day and the Feast of the Purification of the Blessed Virgin'. Dr Joseph Butler, rector from 1769, was also rector of Burham, but on the inheritance of the Milner estates (see above), he lived at Preston Hall. Samuel Bishop, who followed him in 1784 was also rector of a City of London church, St Martin Outwich, and also headmaster of the Merchant Taylors' School in London. Richard Warde, who followed him in 1796 was also vicar of Yalding. Richard Warde's income from the two parishes in 1836 was £298 from Ditton and £1,184 from Yalding. In the era of Jane Austen when the value of a living was most important, these would have given an excellent standard of living when the average agricultural labourer was earning about £40 per year. In the absence of a resident rector, curates were paid, often poorly, to do their work, and among those employed by Richard Warde was Edward Alfree who was also headmaster of Maidstone Grammar School.

Richard Warde had been a curate at Aylesford, where he married Sarah Ramsey in 1790. Sarah's father had been rector of Teston and Nettlestead from 1781-1789. He had formerly worked in the West Indies and his essays on 'The Treatment and Conversion of African Slaves in British Sugar Colonies and An Inquiry into Effects of the Abolition of the Slave Trade' were important catalysts in the anti-slavery movement. The more well-known abolitionists, William Wilberforce and Thomas Clarkson would meet with James Ramsey and others at Teston where they were known as the *Testonites* (Severn, 1975; Hague, 2007). Sarah Warde's mother (Mrs Ramsey) was the daughter of a West Indies Planter, and Sarah would have lived in the West Indies until her father returned home in 1780. She would have rejoiced to see his work come to fruition with the abolition of the slave trade in 1807.

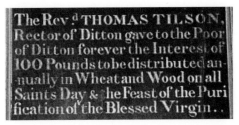

The Revᵈ THOMAS TILSON, Rector of Ditton gave to the Poor of Ditton forever the Interest of 100 Pounds to be distributed annually in Wheat and Wood on all Saints Day & the Feast of the Purification of the Blessed Virgin.

Chapter 7

A Victorian Village: 1837-1901

The hop for his profit I thus doo exalt,
It strengtheneth drinke, and it favoreth malt.

From *Five Hundred Points of Good Husbandry.* Thomas Tusser, 1524-1580

The population of Ditton more than doubled in the first thirty years of the 19th century from 98 in 1801 to 218 in 1831. Even so it was still one of the most sparsely populated parts of the district. In 1831 the population of Aylesford was 1,136, East Malling 1,543 and West Malling 1,459. The increase in Ditton was in part the building of two red brick terraces of houses, one of six houses at Ditton Corner on what was then known as Mill Hall Lane, and called Pleasant Row, and four cottages in Stream Lane, probably on the site of the tanyard. Also recently erected were three or four squatters cottages on Ditton Common. The Common was about 16 acres in extent at the far south east corner of the parish. Squatting was sometimes allowed by the Lord of the Manor, particularly if there was a shortage of agricultural labour. By 1851 there were five cottages on the Common with a total population of 27.

In spite of a gradual rise in population, employment in the parish in the 1840s was still predominantly in agriculture. With the reversion of Mill Hall Mill to flour production in 1833, there were now two corn mills again. However there were three paper mills at East Malling which might have provided some employment. The tanyards at The Stream had closed, and the only commercial outlet was the public house. Parishioners in Ditton would have been totally reliant on the neighbouring villages for most consumer goods. A survey made in 1847 showed that within two to three miles of Ditton in the parishes of Aylesford, and East and West Malling there were 25 inns, taverns or beer houses, 12 blacksmiths, 14 boot and shoe repairers, 8 butchers, 10 grocers, 7 wheelwrights, 6 bakers, 10 tailors, 2 chemists and druggists, 5 surgeons, 2 physicians and 15 builders and carpenters. There were also four watchmakers in West Malling. (Bagshaw, 1847) In addition to these commercial outlets, Maidstone was only about and hour and a half away on foot. There was still a weekly market at West Malling, and annual fairs were held at East Malling on 15th July, and at West Malling on 17th November, St Leonard's Day.

Cottages at Stream Lane, built around 1830. In the centre of the first floor there is still a sign of an insurance company.

Following a relatively settled period of history through the Georgian era, the decade of the 1830s ushered in a number important and far reaching national changes that would affect every parish in England to some extent. There was a significant change in the monarchy with the beginning of the long reign of Victoria in 1837. Changes in parliamentary representation were brought about by the Reform Act of 1832; changes to the responsibility for the poor by the Poor Law Amendment Act of 1834 which created the Union Workhouses; the Constabulary Act of 1832 which created the County Police, although Kent did not establish a County Police until 1857. In the Church of England, the Pluralities Act of 1838 prevented clergy having more than one living located at a distance from each other although adjacent livings were allowed. 1833 marked the beginning of the Oxford Movement, which together with the earlier Evangelical Revival, gave more seriousness of purpose to the majority of clergy. The 1830s also saw the initial building of railways, which would eventually revolutionise communication and transport to an unprecedented extent. By 1844 Maidstone was linked to London by a tortuous rail route via Tonbridge and Redhill! Later in the century elementary schooling would be available for all.

During and following the Napoleonic Wars there was increasing poverty among the agricultural labourers and their families, making the task of the parish Overseer of the Poor even more demanding. In practice, what a farmer did not pay in wages to his workers, he would have to pay as a landowner or tenant farmer in Poor Rate. By 1830 the plight of the labourer was so bad, with the additional threat to their jobs by the use of threshing machines, that riots and machine breaking occurred across Southern England. Collectively known as the *Swing Riots,* they commenced in East Kent in June 1830 and by November had spread across Southern England to Wiltshire (Hobsbawm and Rude, 1969: Matthews, 2006). They were for the demand of a daily wage of 2s..6d in the summer and 2s.3d in the winter. In October 1830 a large wheat rick was set alight at West Peckham, and in early November there was a demonstration meeting by labourers in East Malling. They were led by a Robert Price, and targeted the farm of papermaker Robert Tassell. His labourers did not join in as they were well paid, so they went off to Yalding. Eventually the riots came to an end in 1831 but in England as a whole, 19 rioters were executed and 481 transported. Robert Price was arrested and died in Maidstone Jail before his trial.

The difficulty for individual parishes to maintain adequate care for their poor and needy was recognised, and by the Poor Law Amendment Act of 1834, parishes were grouped together in Unions. A workhouse would be provided and so-called Out Relief given to individuals who remained in their own homes, by the Union relieving officer. The Malling Union, of which Ditton was part, built a workhouse at King Hill, on the road between West Malling and Mereworth. The large red brick buildings were opened in 1836 with a ragstone chapel built in 1872, which functioned as union workhouse until 1929. Each of the individual parishes had a representative on the Board of Guardians that was responsible for the workhouse management. The erstwhile demands on the Poor Rate for a small parish such as Ditton is well illustrated by the case of the Swan family. They were such a cause of major expenditure, that the parish officers compiled an account book of their case over 21 years. Stephen Swan and his wife Sarah and three children were living in Wateringbury. When in 1815, Stephen was ill and unable to work, the Wateringbury officers ordered his removal to his original place of settlement, Ditton, which would then take financial responsibility for the family. Stephen died in 1816, and Sarah in 1818. Three children then aged about ten, eight and three were now the total responsibility of the parish, and care and accommodation were provided for these orphans over the next 16 years until the youngest, Harriet, was married to a farmer from Goudhurst in 1836. From 1815 to 1835, the parish had paid out £260 for the support of the Swan family.

Many of the local members of the Malling Board of Guardians were also Justices of the Peace (Magistrates). Throughout the 18th and early 19th century the magistrates had conducted their business in the Swan Inn in Swan Street, West Malling. With the establishment of the Kent County Police in 1857, the Ditton parish constables handed over their task to a professional force now based in West Malling. In 1866 a new police station and Magistrate's Court were built in what would from then on be called Police Station Road.

The Parliamentary Reform Act of 1832 made very little impact on most Ditton residents. Until the Act many small places, often called *Rotten Boroughs* might send one or two members to Parliament from a very small electorate, whereas the growing industrial centres like Manchester, had few, if any representatives. Before 1832 Ditton electors would have voted for two so-called county seats for most of the rural parts of the county, whereas New Romney had two seats of its own! The reform created two seats for rural West Kent. In an election in 1837, there were three candidates for the seats, Sir William Geary of Oxenhoath, West Peckham, Thomas Law Hodges of Benenden, who had married Rebecca Twisden, and would soon become owner of Borough Court and Ditton Farms, and Sir Edward Filmer of East Sutton. There were six potential electors in Ditton, Thomas Allchin of Church Mill, John Golding of Ditton Place, Richard Pemble tenant of Borough Court, Philip Pusey (of Pusey in Berkshire) owner of Ditton Court, and Richard Warde (rector, resident of Yalding). At that time poll books showed how electors voted. The last two did not vote, and the four Ditton residents both voted for Geary and Filmer. When it came to the count, the number cast were for Sir William Geary 3,584, Thomas Law Hodges 3,334 and Sir Edward Filmer, 3,229. The first two were therefore elected. Six electors from Ditton with a population of 244, two of whom were non resident, was fairly typical of the representation of much of England where an average of about 5% of the adult male population could vote.

We are able to obtain an accurate and detailed picture of crop growth and land use as well as the number employed in agriculture, by linking the information of the tithe award of 1841 with the census of 1851 which gives a detail of occupation. Over the years it was becoming an increasing burden to parochial clergy to collect their tenth of the crop yield (tithe) in produce, thus the Tithe Commutation Act of 1832 made a money payment compulsory. In the next ten or so years surveyors created detailed parish maps, and worked out the amount to be paid for every plot of land. Of the five farms in the parish the approximate area of land was:

Ditton Court Farm (tenant Henry Ranger)	219 acres
Ditton Place Farm (owner John Golding)	119 acres
Ditton Farm (tenant Charles Miles)	93 acres
Borough Court Farm (tenant Richard Pemble)	69 acres
Lone Barn Farm (tenant Thomas Browning)	44 acres
Kiln Barn Farm (tenant Henry Bennet)	25 acres

In addition to gardens and common land, there were 350 acres of woodland. In 1841 the acreage of arable was 381, hops 88, meadow 81 and orchards 23. The arable crops would be predominantly wheat and barley, with some peas, beans and turnips. All of the orchards were in close proximity to the streamside farms and it was not until later in the century that extensive orchards were planted on the Ditton Court Farm at some distance from the farm centre.

In 1851 a major part of the working male population of Ditton was connected with agriculture. The total population of 235 (123 male, 112 female) included three farmers and three baliffs, 48 agricultural/farm labourers, 13 of whom were sons still living at home. In addition there were five waggoners, two mates with horse teams, one shepherd and two shepherd boys aged 10 and 12, and one carter. Ditton Place Farm employed 14 farm labourers and Ditton Court Farm 12. The only other identified male occupation was four carpenters and four unspecified labourers. Of the female population, 14 were employed as domestic servants, exactly at the national average of 12.5%. While the agricultural labourers would have been working for at least 12 hours each day in the summer and as much as light permitted in the winter at ploughing, planting, harvesting, hand threshing, maintaining orchards and hop gardens, the wives and children would often be busily employed as well. A Poor Law Commission report on the employment of women and children in agriculture published in 1841 specifically described work within 10 miles of Maidstone in hop gardens and orchards and in arable crops. These are some examples: women could be employed for ten hours a day on hop planting (opening the hills), helping to secure poles in the ground (poling), tying the plants to the poles, then picking, clearing the hop garden and manuring. Boys as young as eight would help with poling, and then when both boys and girls were 12 years old, they could help with all the other tasks associated with hop growing. From the age of eight boys might be employed for 12 hours each day in hand weeding, and from 12, reaping about a quarter of an acre of corn in two days (Vaughan, 1843).

> Let those who feast at ease on dainty fare,
> Pity the reapers, who their feasts prepare.
>
> From *The Thresher's Labour* ,by Stephen Duck

In the 1830s and 40s the average farm labourer was earning around 10 shillings a week, almost half of which was spent on flour for bread making which could be obtained from either Church or Mill Hall Mills. Small sums were spent on butter, bacon and cheese, and even smaller amounts on soap and candles. Most cottages had reasonably sized gardens enabling them, with the help of their families, to grow a good amount of produce (Tufnell 1847). Towards the end of the 18th century some farmers allowed their workers an extra plot of land for potatoes. In Ditton a six acre plot of land in Kiln Barn Road, later part of the quarry and owned by the Lord of the Manor, was designated in the Tithe Award of 1841 as 'Occupier; Poor of the Parish: Cottage Allotments'. A later map of 1849 shows the division of this land into 16 plots. Another piece of land that all in the parish had the opportunity to make use of was the 22 or so acres of Ditton Common. This had been common land from time immemorial, and although two miles in walking distance from the centre of Ditton, was still a useful source of firewood and potential grazing. Over the years (see above) some cottagers had set up permanent residences there. Edward Betts, the owner of the surrounding land, was keen to incorporate this into his estate. As was the usual procedure, an Act of Parliament in 1852 approved the enclosure which was put into practice in 1859. For three of the squatters, Betts built new two up and two down cottages on the southern edge of the common, calling these 'Perseverance Cottage', 'Summer Place' and 'St Peter's Cottage'. They were demolished in the 1950s. Betts also had to give a monetary compensation to the other parish landowners. Just over one acre of land was kept for parish allotments but this was sold in 1914 for land nearer to the village centre. What is left today of the well maintained Ditton Green is a remnant of common space that was available to all. It is smaller than it was two hundred years ago due to new roads and school building, but the parish quarry and the pound have both vanished. The pound, for confining stay animals, is clearly marked on a map of 1849 between two pairs of cottages on the east side of The Green.

Ditton Rectory in Kiln Barn road as built in 1842. A photograph taken in 1955. This house was demolished after a fire while empty in 1970.

With the death of the Rev'd Richard Warde in 1840, a long incumbency of 44 years came to an end. He lived at Yalding where he is commemorated in a large memorial, so his presence an influence in Ditton must have been rather limited. Although he contributed to the purchase of the organ in 1814, the churchwardens' accounts for 1815 state 'The Rev'd Mr Warde has promised to give annually toward the playing of the organ £1.1.0'. Below this there is cryptic note in pencil, *But never paid any money.* Since Mr Warde had been appointed the Pluralities Act had come into force, and Ditton would have a resident rector for many years with the appointment of the Irish born Rev'd William Hamilton Burroughs, whose stipend was £298 per annum. The old thatched rectory was now clearly inadequate, and was demolished. On the site in 1842 was built a large new red brick rectory, with at least eight bedrooms and servants' quarters in the attic. A large tank was constructed below ground and fed by rain water from the roof, as its major water supply. The grounds, with a stable and coach house, were laid out as a 'gentleman's' residence with many trees, including acacia and cedar and extensive lawns. At the census of 1851 William Burroughs lived in this large residence with two house servants and one house and garden labourer. On that census day 31st March 1851, the only national census of church attendance in England was also taken. With a population of 235 and no competing non-conformist chapels, the attendance at morning service in St Peter's Church was only 10 (4.2%) and in the afternoon 25 (10.6%). This is a very low attendance, and might reflect the many years of an absence of a resident clergyman. The National average for attending an Anglican church was over 20% of the population. Aylesford Church on the same day had attendances of 280 (18%) in the morning, and 340 (22%) in the afternoon (Roake, 1999). Although the attendance at St Peter's Church was small, the church could seat a good percentage of the parish, if needed, as shown by a seating survey.

Seating in St Peter's Church, Ditton, 1851:

	Poor	Children	Other	Total
Nave	32	26	47	105
Gallery	53		3	56
Total	**85**	**26**	**50**	**161**

Ten years previously in 1841 the Archdeacon of Rochester had made a number of comments about the poor state of the decorative order of the church. 'The interior of the church and chancel requires cleaning and whitewashing, and the pew in the chancel and the rails round the communion table to be painted. The vestry room to be painted and whitewashed. To paint the outer door of the church.' There are drawings of the exterior of the church by the well known topographical artist John Claude Nattes (1765-1822) who visited the village on July 31st 1816 and made two drawings of the church and two of Church Mill. These show the exterior of the building much as we know it today, apart from a porch on the south side which was the main church entrance. The vestry was then the room at the base of the tower. The large east window is shown by Nattes to be in Wren style with no tracery, but this was inserted in 1843. The pew in the chancel mentioned by the archdeacon would have been a 'communicants pew' where those taking communion on the rare occasions of celebration, would sit.

A drawing of St Peter's Church by J.C. Nattes in 1816. This shows the church before a major restoration in 1859 that included the removal of the south porch. In the background is the old Ditton Court.

When the rector William Burroughs died in 1856, a new chapter was opened in the life of St Peter's Church, the parish of Ditton and various organisations in the County of Kent. The new rector was the socially concerned and dynamic John Young Stratton. He came from a Lancashire curacy, but was Cambridge educated and remained as rector until his death in 1905. He immediately set about a re-seating and restoration of the church, and described how 'the greater part of the ground space is occupied by large pews appropriated to certain families, the remainder being open benched for the poor, most insufficient to accommodate them, while the pews are comparatively unoccupied'. In addition to re-pewing in 1859, the chosen architect, the eminent Sir George Gilbert Scott (1811-1878), designed a new chancel arch to replace a Norman one, two new windows for the south of the nave, and blocked the main south door. One of the corbels of the arch has a carving of hops! The whole project cost just over £300 of which £50 was contributed by the major land owner and Lord of the Manor, Edward Betts of Preston Hall, £50 by the Earl of Aylesford, patron of the living, and £50 by John Stratton himself. The new pulpit and lectern were given by the Luck family, long associated with Ditton Court. Five years before the restoration of St.Peter's Church, a new church, Holy Trinity, had been built between Larkfield and New Hythe, only about two hundred yards from the Ditton border. Perhaps these Anglican developments had in part been motivated by the thought of competing non-conformity by the building of a Baptist Chapel at West Malling in 1836, and Methodist Chapels at East Malling in 1844 and Aylesford in 1851.

A corbel of the new chancel arch of 1859 with hops

Coming to work in a rural parish dominated by agriculture, John Stratton became increasingly concerned with the life and economic status of the agricultural labourer. In 1864 he wrote a lengthy article on 'The Life of a Farm Labourer' for the *Cornhill Magazine* (Stratton, 1864). The New Poor Law with Union Workhouses had been established only 30 years ago, and Stratton recognised their important role for the homeless and destitute, but thought that 'it has no right to tear family ties in pieces, at the moment distress drives the objects of its care within its fold: so that husband and wife, parent and child, must learn to forget one another, and be left in their loneliness and misery'. This article and a subsequent one in the Journal of the Royal Agricultural Society (Stratton, 1870) advanced the case for the security and support of a large Friendly Society, rather than the small village societies. He was one of the leading protagonists of the County of Kent Friendly Society which had been founded in 1822. Living in the centre of a large hop growing area, Stratton also saw the poor living conditions that visiting hop pickers had. He was instrumental in setting up a committee to improve the standard of hopper huts, to help with transport from London, to provide provisions for the pickers, and to assist in mission work among them. His ideas were encapsulated in a book *Hops and Hop-Pickers* which was published by SPCK (Stratton, 1883).

The Rev'd John Stratton, rector of Ditton from 1856 to 1905, in his study at Ditton Place

The Victorian age is renowned as a period when the industrial revolution created a new class of self made nouveau riches. One such was Edward Ladd Betts (1815-1872) who in 1848 became Lord of the Manor of Ditton, and owner of 650 acres of the parish. Betts was born in 1815 near Dover, where his father was a civil engineer. He worked with the outstanding engineer Robert Stephenson on some major railway projects, and in 1847 formed a partnership with Samuel Peto. By this time he had become a wealthy man, and as his partner, and now brother in law, Peto, had just purchased and enlarged Somerleyton, a mansion in Suffolk, he clearly wished to follow his example. Preston Hall and its estate of nearly three thousand acres was purchased from Henry Milner in 1848, and he almost immediately demolished the old Tudor/Jacobean mansion of the Colepepers. Betts employed the same architect as Peto, John Thomas, who was more renowned for his sculptures than his architecture, to build a new mansion in the Jacobean style. The new Preston Hall was completed by 1857, and built of locally quarried ragstone with Caen stone dressings. It was constructed on a palatial scale with conspicuous towers and chimneys and extensive stabling, gardens and lodges, laundry and gas works (Sephton, 1997). An avenue of cedar trees ran along what was know as 'Green Drive' from the house south to Broke Wood on the edge of Ditton Common. One drive continued into the chestnut coppice of Oaken Wood in Ditton, while another cut back at an acute angle through Deadman Wood to the peak of Holt Wood. This avenue was lined with cedar trees, monkey puzzles and rhododendrons, some of which remain to this day. He re-organised the layout of the sweet chestnut coppices in Oaken Wood, which were well placed to provide the local hop growers with poles. On the top of Holt Hill a stone built summer house with a thatched roof was erected just inside the Ditton border. Here Edward Betts was truly 'lord of all he surveyed.' In Pratling Street, Aylesford, he established a pottery and brickworks that utilised local sand. For a while his railway construction business prospered with major projects in Denmark,

HOPS AND HOP-PICKERS.

BY THE

REV. J. Y. STRATTON,

RECTOR OF DITTON, KENT;

AUTHOR OF "SUGGESTIONS FOR LEGISLATION RELATING TO FRIENDLY
SOCIETIES," ETC.

OAST-HOUSE AT DITTON, KENT.

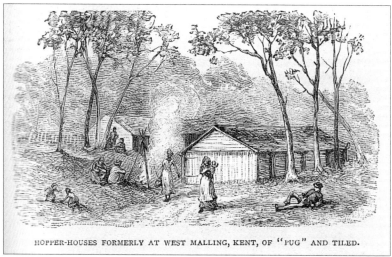

HOPPER-HOUSES FORMERLY AT WEST MALLING, KENT, OF "PUG" AND TILED.

*Extract from title page and two illustrations from John Stratton's
book* Hops and Hop-Pickers. *Centre: Oast-house at Ditton,
Kent; Below: Hopper houses at West Malling.*

Australia and America. In 1856 they constructed the new line from Strood to Maidstone for the South Eastern Railway (SER), giving a more direct route from Maidstone to London. This line crossed some low lying fields of Borough Court Farm near the River Medway to Mill Hall, where Aylesford Station was constructed. The station building and crossing gate lodge at Aylesford were built in the Jacobean style of his mansion. Ditton residents now had a railway station a short walk from the village, with all its possibilities for travel, and transport. By 1858 Betts was a magistrate, Deputy Lieutenant and High Sheriff of Kent, but in 1865 he failed in his bid to be the Conservative M.P. for Maidstone. A year later a national banking crisis left his company in a serious financial state, and in 1867 he sold the whole of the Preston Hall Estate to an even more renowned railway engineer, Thomas Brassey (1805-1870). When Betts died in 1871 he was buried in Aylesford, and obituaries of him commented on his indomitable energy, general benevolence and warmth of friendship. A memorial fountain in Aylesford erected in 1868 commemorated 'the many acts of kindness conferred on this parish and neighbourhood by Edward Ladd Betts'.

Preston Hall. Designed by John Thomas and built between 1850 and 1857. This photograph was taken in 1887.

Edward Betts' link with Preston Hall, Aylesford and the Ditton area, albeit brief (19 years), left a significant legacy. The mansion of Preston Hall, although not used as a private home for almost one hundred years, still impresses by its size and spectacular roofscape, and by many remnants of estate buildings and landscape planting. In 1853 he paid for the erection of the first village school in Ditton. This was on the edge of The Green on the site of the parish Poor House. It consisted of one room approximately 27 x 16 feet in size with a bellcote, and a Headteacher's house attached. It was possibly designed by the Maidstone architect E.W. Stephens, who in the same year had built a school in Aylesford also for Edward Betts. It was affiliated to the Church of England and called *A National School for Boys and Girls*. Prior to this time educational provision for any children of the 'working classes' from Ditton had been provided for by a foundation set up by the Rev'd Edward Holme, Vicar of Birling from 1756- 1782. Two schools were built, one on the road between Leybourne and Birling in 1775, and another at Clare Lane, East Malling in 1781. The East Malling school could take up to six boys from Ditton and 44 from East Malling. On the school building is an epitaph in Greek and Latin which translated, states 'to improve children with good letters and with piety' and in English 'This house and school, and that at Leybourne were both erected at the sole expense of the Reverend Edward Holme, Vicar of Birling'. The Reverend John Wesley, the founder of the Methodist Church, was a good friend of Edward Holme, and was a trustee of these schools until his death in 1791.

House in Clare Lane, East Malling, once a school founded by the Rev'd Edward Holme

We can glean a picture of the happenings in Ditton School from the Log Books that date from 1863. When National Schools were receiving grants, the keeping of a Log was obligatory from 1862. The head teacher had to make 'the briefest entry that will suffice to specify ordinary progress or whatever other fact…may otherwise deserve to be recorded'. In these early years when Miss Naish was Headmistress, the number of pupils attending varied between 19 and 29. An Inspector's report in 1864 described it as 'a small rural school half infants. The writing, reading, and needlework are much improved. Religious knowledge still backward. The children appeared little accustomed to oral examination'. At this time schooling was not compulsory, and those who came paid one penny each week. Forster's Education Act of 1870 was a recognition by the state of the need for compulsory education for all, and for state support, it was the Education Act of 1880 that made schooling compulsory for all children up to the age of 10. This was raised to 11 in 1893, and 12 in 1899. After 1880 there was a tremendous increase in the population of the parish, but in the first 30 years one room was adequate to cope with numbers of up to 50. The Log Books from the early years refer to absences due to farm work, and even after the introduction of compulsory education the headmistress had difficulty in enforcing attendance (Yates, Hume and Hastings, 1994).

July, 1863 Cherry gathering, girls kept at home to mind little ones.

August, 1863. School closed for 6 weeks, the gathering of hops commences next week.

April, 1865. very small attendance, boys working in the fields.

May, 1878. Several children absent while their parents are hop tying.

August, 1878. Five weeks holiday (hopping).

October, 1878. Attendance 36 children out of 50 on the books; several of the elder boys at work in the potato fields.

July, 1882. Children kept away very much during fruit picking.

There were a number of welcome and unwelcome visitors at the school. For example Mrs Betts, wife of the donor of the school visited in 1863, and her companion, a Mrs Green, gave a talk on 'God our Father'. A few days later the children were invited to visit Preston Hall. The rector, John Stratton, often visited two to three times each week, and in 1870 the children had a 'half holiday and a treat in celebration of Rev. J.G. Stratton's wedding' to Anne Taylor of Boughton Place. When pupil Harry Bonner was kept in 'his mother came and spoke in a very unbecoming manner!'

Between the years 1850 and 1870 residents of Ditton not only saw the building of Preston Hall by a national magnate, but also major changes at Ditton Farm, Ditton Place and Ditton Court, as small scale business people and farmers aspired to be Victorian gentlemen! All three houses are beside the stream, and in each case its features were incorporated into the pleasure gardens. In 1850 Robert Tassell and Henry Smith, who had been his partners since 1838, handed over the running of their three papermills in East Malling to Thomas and George Busbridge. Tassell was now 65 years-old, and on 'retirement' purchased Ditton Farm and Mill Hall Mill in Ditton from Thomas Law Hodges with the objective of making a small 'gentleman's' estate. It is possible that this had been an ambition for some time, as he had purchased some fields near Mill Hall Mill in 1832. Tassell had been born in Maidstone in 1784 and was Mayor and Chief Magistrate in 1823 and 1829. He had set up a business in Maidstone in 1815 as a grocer and cheesemonger, and then in 1821 purchased three paper mills at East Malling as well as farmland.

Cobdown House, built in 1856. Photogaph taken in 2010. Inset: Robert Tassell, 1784-1874. The owner of paper mills at East Malling and the builder of Cobdown House.

The new house in Ditton was constructed on the south side of Cobdown Hill in 1856, and Tassell moved from his house, Blacklands, in East Malling. Appropriately he called the house, Cob Down House, and it was set within a newly landscaped park. A footpath which had crossed Budland (Buckland) Field was diverted, and a new drive with lodge gate was made from near Ditton Corner to the house. Extensive tree planting was made in the new park and on parts of Cobdown Hill where a summer house was erected. Some of the newly introduced Wellingtonia trees were planted where they are now reaching a 150 year-old maturity! Tassell also made major changes to his farm in response to the demand for hops. Between 1800 and 1870 the acreage of hops grown in Kent doubled, with a particular acceleration after 1862 because of the removal of the hop excise duty. This was paralleled by the construction of hundreds of oast houses. Hop poles, used at about 3,500 per acre, could be obtained from the local coppice woods, and a creosote works had been established in 1860 on the bank of the River Medway near New Hythe to provide a wood preservative for the hop poles. The oasts at Cobdown Farm were built in the 1860s, with four red brick, round drying kilns, and a large two storied cooling and storage chamber. In 1863 he built a row of four red brick cottages for his workers, next to the farm. Robert Tassell lived long enough to see his retirement career flourish; he died in 1874 at the age of 89 having made a considerable impression on the landscape and buildings of Ditton.

Cobdown Farm oast houses taken across the former parkland of Cobdown House in 2010

John Golding of Ditton Place died in 1856 at the age of 85. With his death Ditton Place was sold, and a 150 year link with this family came to an end. For the last 22 years after the death of his wife, he had living in the house a groom,

Cobdown Farm Cottages, built in 1863

A late Victorian cottage scene 'Preparing for Dinner' in the kitchen of a Cobdown Farm Cottage. Painted by John Dodge (1868-1957) around 1880. The painting includes his mother, Jane (1838-1927), sisters Elizabeth and Mercy, and brother Joseph.

a farm bailiff, and three servants. His eldest son William was a clergyman in Somerset, and John had outlived all his other children, including Clementina who had married Alfred Luck of The Hermitage, West Malling, and Caroline who had married Robert Tassell junior of Cobdown. Ditton Place and farm were purchased by Septimus Maitland in 1857. Maitland was a Jamaica-born London tea merchant, and with the opening of the station at Aylesford might have been the first commuter from Ditton to London! He soon initiated a plan to rebuild the house and farm. Almost in imitation of Robert Tassell at Cobdown, he converted a paddock on the ground towards Bradbourne Lane into parkland. He initiated an ambitious tree planting scheme with a carefully planned arrangement of sweet chestnut, horse chestnut and sycamore trees, with some clumps of beech and Scots pine. Like Tassell, he planted a number of more exotic conifers nearer to the house. A new drive was made with a thatched lodge gate almost opposite the entrance to Bell Lane. He changed the character of the stream, by inserting small waterfalls and a spectacular cascade by the London Road. He instigated a rebuilding of John Golding's farm buildings, and erected right on the London Road a large oasthouse with six kilns. Maitland's desire for more privacy had the most far reaching effect on the village. He obtained permission to close Ditton Street, the major route from The Green area to the London Road that passed behind his house and a new road, *New Road*, was constructed to run directly from The Green to Ditton Corner. Ditton Corner thus became a cross roads.

Ditton Place as rebuilt around 1860. This house was demolished after a fire while empty in 1987.

A map of Ditton surveyed in 1864, and published by the Ordnance Survey in 1869

Edward Betts sold the Preston Hall estate, including Ditton Court and the Lordship of the Manor of Ditton to Thomas Brassey in 1867. Both Betts and Peto had worked with Brassey on major railway and dock schemes in Canada and England. Brassey was associated with the construction of over nineteen hundred miles of railways in Britain, and when he died he was described as the wealthiest self-made Victorian. He was also affected by the banking crisis that destroyed Betts' business in 1866, and lost over a million pounds. Although Thomas Brassey did not live in Preston Hall, it was left to his second surviving son Henry Arthur Brassey (1840-1891). Like Betts before him, Henry Brassey was High Sheriff of Kent in 1890, but unlike Betts he did get elected to Parliament, as MP for Sandwich from 1868-85. Under his ownership the estate prospered, and was enlarged to over four thousand acres, 650 of which were in Ditton.

A major project in the early 1870s was to turn Ditton Court into a model farm for a gentleman farmer. Throughout England landed gentry were proudly making considerable investments in their tenant farms using the latest technology with materials which could be brought in by rail. The only known picture of the old farmhouse of Ditton Court is a not very revealing sketch in the background of a drawing of 1816. The new eight-bedroomed brick building would be very different; it was three stories high, with high late-Victorian type gables and prominent chimney stacks. The so-called 'Pleasure Gardens' included two tennis courts and a croquet lawn. Most of the old farm buildings, including an oast house with three kilns, were next to the house. These were progressively demolished over a number of years as a suite of modern farm buildings was erected about two hundred yards away, on the edge of The Green. Like much of the Preston Hall estate buildings of the time, the new farm was constructed of locally quarried ragstone with yellow brick dressings and slate roofs. The buildings surrounded two large yards with extensive stabling for 15 horses, cow sheds for 24 cows, and a large three kiln oast house with the latest style of square kilns. Integral to the buildings was a bailiff's office, an engine house for a stationary steam engine to drive machinery, a granary and a number of cart sheds. Later in the century, and linked to the model farm, were five new four roomed cottages, built in pairs on Kiln Barn Road, all single storey apart from the farm bailiff's two-storeyed house.

The settled nature of a small agricultural community which, with additional farm cottages, had reached modest population of 336 by 1881 (Aylesford 2719, East Malling 2,383, West Malling 2,242) was to change out of all recognition in the next ten years. Industrial developments across the River Medway were to have considerable influence, leading to a rise in population of 874 by 1891. Ditton would never again be a small village linked only to farming and the land.

The rapid increase in the population of London in the first half of the 19th

Ditton Court as rebuilt around 1870. This photograph was taken from the church tower in 1960. The house was demolished in 1972.

Ditton Court Farm cottages in Kiln Barn Road in 2010. The furthest house was the bailiff's residence.

century demanded an increase in house building and thus building materials. The Lower Medway valley between Aylesford and the Thames estuary had the raw materials for cement and brick manufacture, and good transport access by river to London. Edward Betts had established a brick, tile and pottery works in Aylesford parish in the 1840s, and by the middle of the 1850s there was a very large brickworks at Burham, with cement works attached, established by Thomas Cubitt a well-known architect and developer. Even nearer to Ditton on the opposite bank of the River Medway from New Hythe was another extensive brickworks. In time a number of cement works were constructed in Wouldham, Snodland and Halling. These developments were reflected in the increase in population between 1851 and 1871 of the erstwhile rural parishes of Burham and Wouldham, and of Aylesford with the development of the hamlet of Eccles. (Preston, 1977; Hann, 2009):

Year	1841	1851	1861	1871	1881	1891
Burham	380	518	775	1,172	1,353	1,680
Wouldham	284	343	433	818	1,268	1,373
Aylesford	1,344	1,487	2,057	2,100	2,719	2,979
Ditton	**244**	**235**	**255**	**287**	**336**	**874**

The effect of these industrial changes was also felt in Ditton, but about twenty years later than in these other parishes. It was not until around 1880, following ownership changes, that land was available for house building. In 1876 Septimus Maitland left Ditton Place to live nearer to London in Bexley, and the house was sold to the rector, John Stratton. After letting the house for some years, in the 1890s he moved into the large house and let out the rectory in Kiln Barn Road. Whereas Maitland had been a farmer, especially of hops, Stratton rented out the farm land, but in a short time sold a number of pieces of land for development. This was a few years after the influential Public Health Act of 1875 which *inter alia* set a higher standard for house building and sanitation. As piped water was not available in Ditton at this time, the new houses were built with terraces sharing a well with a pump, and the provision of earth closets towards the

A plaque on Bell Cottages in New Road

rear of the gardens. Land to the west of New Road was built on between 1881-1884, including Fair View Cottages (1881), Sunnyside, Bell Cottages and Daisy Bank (1882), Maida Place and Rocky Bank (1883). Around the corner on the London Road the large house (Ditton Holme) and Grand View were built in 1884. Bell Field, a large hop garden between Bell Lane and the stream at Cobdown was developed in the next few years.

London Road, Ditton Nr. Maidstone.

Houses in the London Road built in the 1880s. A picture taken around 1920 before road widening in 1927. From the left: Belmont, Jubilee Terrace, Gordon Terrace, Khartoum Terrace and Cascade Villas.

On the London Road three of the rows of houses had significant contemporary names. In 1885, General Gordon, the Governor of Sudan had been killed in Khartoum, thus two rows were called Gordon Terrace (1886), and Khartoum Terrace (1886). The following year was the Golden Jubilee of Queen Victoria, and the next houses were therefore called Jubilee Terrace (1887). Of the numerous houses built in Ditton during this decade, this is the only terrace with a builder's name, 'E. Santco, builders', were a London-based firm. A row of houses, including two shops were Cascade Cottages as at that time the stream from Ditton Place cascaded in a picturesque waterfall on the opposite side of the road. A new road, now Orchard Grove was destined for extensive development, but only six houses were built at that time, Waterlow Cottages, and Edith Villas. The east side and bottom of Bell Lane saw the greatest development including Alma Place, Ferndale Cottages, Maida Place, Arrow Cottages, Vine Cottages, Annington

Terrace, Belmont Cottages, Payne's Cottages and Johnson's Cottages. Since the 1851 census, a public house, The Walnut Tree, had been built at the London Road end of Bradbourne Lane. The landlord, Henry Humphreys had seven sons, four of whom were employed in cement manufacture, but Edward, then aged nine would subsequently achieve fame as a Kent County cricketer. Known by the nickname 'Punter', he played in over 360 first-class games for Kent between 1899 and 1920. This was a golden period for Kent cricket. They won the county championship four times between 1900 and 1913, and Punter would have played with such stars as Frank Woolley and Tich Freeman.

 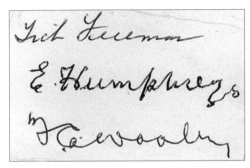

Autograph of the cricketer Ted (Punter) Humphreys together with two Kent and England notable players. From the author's autograph book of 1949.

In addition to the numerous terraces built in the 1880s, a large detached house was built on a 16 acre field called Crow Plane between the west side of Bell Lane and the London Road. This house, Fernleigh, was built by Samuel Lee Smith of the nearby Larkfield Hall. It became the home of the Boorman family, with Thomas Boorman described in the census of 1891 as 'Portland Cement Manufacturer', with works at Cuxton. Lee Smith, who eventually purchased Borough Court and Cobdown House and farm, was the co-owner of cement works at Snodland. (Referred to at that time as 'Cementopolis'). His grandfather, William Lee, had evolved from being a lime producer to a cement manufacturer, and in the process had amassed a fortune, also becoming MP for Maidstone.

The major increase in the population of Ditton between 1880 and 1890, with the building of these many terraces and houses, and with the development of cement, brick and pottery industries within easy access in the Medway valley, is reflected in male employment at the time of the 1891 census. In 1851 around 60 men were employed in agriculture, with four unspecified labourers. Now in 1891 there were still around sixty employed in agriculture, but there were also 62 described as 'general labourer' (possibly taking seasonal work, when available, on farm, quarry or factory) and 29 specifically as *labourer, cement works*. For the first time in its long history agriculture had lost its place as the predominant employment of Ditton parish residents. Now many of these workers would daily cross the River Medway at the New Hythe ferry. One employee, William Barrell of Fair View, New Road, was a bargemaster, and the school log-book for 1887 noted that 'The Barrells away with their father on his barge for several weeks'.

A comparison of the census returns for 1851 and 1891 give an indication of an increasing and more mobile population. The number of children in many families was rising, and there was a gradual drift from the land to industrial employment, often to improved housing conditions. Whereas 112 (48%) of the Ditton residents in 1851 had been born in the parish, this had risen to 215 in 1891, but was now only 25% of the total population; 111(13%) were from East Malling, and 74 (8 %) were from Aylesford. In 1851 only 8 (3%) had been born out of Kent, but by 1891 this was 120 (13%). Other local places which were the birthplace of more than ten Ditton residents in 1891, included Maidstone (34), West Malling (17), Wrotham (13), Burham (14), Wouldham (12), Barming (10) and Hunton (10). Between 1874 and 1896 there was a great depression in agriculture in England, caused in part by some bad seasonal weather, an increase in foreign competition and some national monetary policy. Nationally one-third of agricultural labourers left the land in these years, some to industrial work and some by emigration. One farm labourer from Cobdown Farm, Ditton, left to work in the newly opened gold mines of Charters Towers in Queensland, Australia. He was killed in a mine accident in 1909.

The repercussions of the building of 120 or so houses and the population change from 336 to 874 in ten years, were considerable. Realising that St Peter's Church would be too small for such a population, Miss Catherine Tassell, a daughter of Robert Tassell of Cobdown, donated in 1891 a tin Mission Room on the west side of Bell Lane. This was subsequently moved to the east side. Faced with a sudden increase in potential school children, who by now had a right to education to the age of ten, a large additional schoolroom was donated by Henry Brassey of Preston Hall. The Log Book for April 1887 noted 'The enlargement of the school; premises commenced'. On May 27th 'The Memorial stone of the new school room laid on Thursday at noon by Miss Brassey. A bottle with writings enclosed placed in the cavity behind the stone by the Rev, J.G. Stratton'. The generosity of the Brassey family is still recorded on the wall tablet: **This School was enlarged by H.A. BRASSEY, Esq.,in commemoration of the Jubilee year of Queen Victoria's reign.** By July 1st 1887 the Log Book noted 'Re-opened school in the New School Room. Found it very pleasant and airy'. A few weeks later to celebrate Victoria's Golden Jubilee 132 children were taken to Preston Hall for a treat 'in wagons lent by Mr Scott' (farmer of Ditton Court). In 1891 Frank Bartholomew came to the newly enlarged school as Headmaster, and remained for over 30 years. The former head, Miss Charlotte Neath then took charge of the infants department. A separate Infants School was built on The Green and on

Jan 8th 1894 'The infants took possession of their New Room'. With numbers of children rising, Mr Bartholomew wrote in 1892 'for the first time in history of this school, I had 100 children present during the morning. In honour of the event the children were dismissed at 11.50, each receiving a new slate pencil as they left the room'. By 1894 with the infants' department fully functional there were sometimes 167 children present out of a possible 190 on the books. Outbreaks of infectious diseases are reported, such as the outbreak of Typhoid Fever in 1884 which claimed the life of the church organist Mr Wallis. Children from the school sang at his funeral in St Peter's Church. The increasing prevalence of outbreaks of infectious diseases led to the establishment by the District Council of an isolation (fever) hospital not far from the Ditton boundary at Kiln Barn at Rocks Road, East Malling. This closed in 1947, and is now Four Acres.

Ditton, Kent.

Ditton School around 1900. The first schoolroom with the bell turret was built in 1853, with a teacher's house attached. The larger schoolroom to the left was built in 1887.

With the coming of the railways, Turnpike Trusts lost considerable revenue, and following legislation, were taken over by Highway Boards. Their duties also embraced all parish roads which had been the responsibility of parish waywardens. Thus the London Road turnpike and all other parish roads became the responsibility of the Malling Highway Board from 1864 until 1888, when County Highway Authorities were set up. The coming of the North Kent Line of the South Eastern Railway through Ditton in 1856, as it followed a course to Maidstone and then to Tonbridge, must have diminished the amount of freight conveyed on the River Medway, although the siting of the line on the west bank of the River Medway would eventually prove to be a major disadvantage for the Burham brick and cement works. The meandering nature of the Medway between Aylesford and Halling led to silting problems, some of which were alleviated by making new cuts across a 'meander'. In 1845 The Medway Navigation Company made a new cut called 'The Middle Cut' across the most northerly part of Ditton. This left about 15 acres of land which was owned in part by the Preston Hall estate, and by Thomas Law Hodges, totally detached from the parish. In course of time this was linked to Aylesford Parish, and in recent years has been known as The Island Site. To complete the major transport changes of the 19th century, the London Chatham and Dover Railway (LCDR) created a link to Maidstone in 1874 from a junction at Otford on their line from Swanley to Sevenoaks. Ten years later, in 1884 this line was extended from Maidstone to Ashford, and thus provided an alternative route from the Channel ports to London. For only half a mile this line cut across Kiln Field, New Gate Field and Lower Knoxes on an embankment, before entering a deep cutting to a tunnel under the ornamental drives of Preston Hall. The competitive nature of the two lines through Kent, the SER and the LCDR meant that most towns like Maidstone had two lines and two stations. From 1899 they worked together as the South Eastern and Chatham Railway (SECR), or as the locals called it, 'The Slow Easy and Comfortable Railway!'

Major local government changes took place within the county and within the parish in the latter years of the 19th century. The first meeting of the Kent County Council took place at the Sessions House in Maidstone in 1889. This had evolved from the Court of General Session which had consisted of justices of the peace. The first councillor for the Malling area was Samuel Lee Smith of Larkfield. He served on the council for 34 years: 25 as an elected member, and nine as a county alderman. The Local Government Act of 1894 led to the establishment of Parish Councils. They took over the civil functions of the Vestry which retained the ecclesiastical responsibilities until the formation of Parochial Church Councils in 1922. A meeting to form a parish council was held in Ditton School in December 1894 and was chaired by the rector. Thomas Scott from Ditton Court Farm was elected as the first chairman and other members included his farm bailiff James Gardiner, George Smart who followed him as bailiff, Walter Skinner of Mill Hall Mill, Henry Humphries of the Walnut Tree, and William Williamson who ran the Working Men's Club in New Road. The clerk was Silas Wagon a farmer and sand pit owner from Aylesford, who held this post until 1913. One of the early tasks of the council was to introduce some street lighting. In 1897 they purchased 12 cast iron columns, each with a ladder bracket and 50 candle power lantern. The arrangements for lighting were set out as 'one hour after sunset and to be put out at 10.30pm on every night of the week, except Saturday, when they are to be put out at 11 o'clock. For seven night at full moon the lamps are not to be lit'. Lighting only continued to the middle of April each year. The oil lamps were replaced by gas in 1912.

As the 19th century came towards an end, Queen Victoria celebrated her Diamomd Jubilee, and a new bell was purchased for St Peter's Church with the inscription *Victoria R.I. 1897*. When Victoria died in 1901 the population had risen in the previous century from 98 to a nine fold increase of 885.

Oak-apple Day, May 29th 1900, on the lawn of Ditton Place. Some ladies of the village with the Rev'd John Stratton, centre front, with his daughters Frances and Mabel. Behind Mr Stratton is the curate Mr H.B.C. Collins. This day was the commemoration of the Restoration of Charles II in 1660. It was a traditional custom to wear oak leaves.

Chapter 8

War and Peace: 1900-1950

There were poured out, in constant attack and counterattack, millions of lives and the accumulated wealth of the past century of European progress.

A Shortened History of England. G.M. Trevelyan, 1876-1962

The 20th century began with the Nation at war. The latest war with the Boers in South Africa had begun in 1899, but unlike the later major conflicts of the new century it was far removed from most people. Like the naming of 'Gordon' and 'Khartoum Terraces' in Ditton a few years earlier, National pride was shown by the name 'Mafeking Cottages' for two cottages built in Larkfield in 1900. In the next year Queen Victoria died and at the Coronation of Edward VII the Lord of the Manor of Ditton, Mr H.L.C. Brassey M.P., entertained the children and old people of Ditton, Aylesford and Allington to a celebration at Preston Hall. His wife, Lady Violet, the daughter of the Duke of Richmond apparently had little affection for Preston Hall, and they moved to the impressive Tudor mansion of Apethorpe in Northamptonshire in 1904, where he was subsequently ennobled as Lord Brassey of Apethorpe. Most of the four thousand or more acres of the estate were soon put up for sale. The Ditton Court Farm estate of nearly four hundred acres together with Church Mill and the mill house, were purchased by the tenant farmer, Thomas Scott in 1905. Mr Scott was one of a number of Scottish farmers who came to Kent to farm at the end of the 19th century. Others included the Mitchells of Ryarsh then Wateringbury, and the Westons of Rocks Farm, East Malling. They had been tempted south by the competitive land rents that were available towards the end of the agricultural depression that lasted until 1896 (Protheroe, 1936).

Mr Scott had a particular interest in hop and fruit growing, and he extended his fruit plantations with extensive areas of apples, pears, plums and cherries, as well as red and black currants, gooseberries, strawberries and cobnuts. It is not surprising therefore, that when the Wye College Fruit Experimental Station was looking for a suitable piece of land to study 'the problems met with in the actual

A ploughing match at Ditton Court Farm in 1910. The plough is a traditional wooden Kentish turn-wrest plough. Unlike the 19th century metal ploughs with a fixed mouldboard, the wrest or mouldboard could be fixed to the plough to right or left.

culture of trees and bushes,' Mr Scott offered them 23 acres of his field Great East situated in the parishes of Ditton and East Malling. Thus what was to become the East Malling Research Station was established and with the considerable support of Kent fruit growers, funds were raised to erect a laboratory, office and stable building in 1914. Unfortunately, Thomas Scott died in July 1913 at the age of 57 without seeing the progress of the research work and the establishment of an institute with a world-wide reputation. His death was a great loss to the parish. He had been an efficient and popular Chairman of the Parish Council for nearly 20 years: he had been instrumental in the establishment of the Institute and Working Men's Club in New Road, and had founded a scout group in the village soon after the publication of Baden-Powel's *Scouting for Boys* in 1908. The school log book for July 13th 1913 says 'three members of the Boy Scout Troup were absent to attend the funeral of the late Thomas Scott, a manager of the school'.

A few years earlier in 1905, the Rector, John Stratton had died suddenly at the age of 75. He had been Rector of Ditton for 48 years, a most caring and influential man, and his passing was acutely felt. At a Parish meeting a resolution was passed expressing 'the deep sorrow the parish has sustained by the death of the rector, who for the greater part of his lifetime has been its rector, who was so universally esteemed and respected by his parishioners, and also to express their appreciation of the service he has rendered to the parish'. A few years later in 1910, the east window of St Peter's Church with glass by the firm of Kempe and Tower, was dedicated to his memory.

LOT 5.

ALL THAT VERY HIGHLY CULTIVATED

FREEHOLD FARM

COLOURED PINK ON THE PLAN,

Situate in the Parishes of Ditton and Aylesford. It possesses very long frontages to the Ditton and East Malling Road, and, in addition, is conveniently intersected with excellent accommodation roads. It comprises the well-appointed and comfortably arranged

GABLED RESIDENCE

KNOWN AS

"DITTON COURT,"

surrounded by attractive

PLEASURE GARDENS,

COMPANY'S WATER is laid on to the House and **GAS** is available.

Situate at a convenient distance from the Residence, and adjoining the East Malling Road, are the Modern, Substantial and very complete Stone-built and Slated

RANGE OF FARM BUILDINGS.

They comprise 8-stalled Stable, Harness Room, 7-stall Stable with Loose Box and Harness Room, Bailiff's Office with Weighbridge and Tool House with 2 large Stores over, Nag Stable containing 2 Loose Boxes and Stall, Harness Room, Coach House with Tank Roof, Cow House for 24 Cows, Dairy, Engine House, Grinding Room, Loft over, Hay Loft and Chaff Store, 3 large Loose Boxes, 4-bay Wagon Lodge, with Carpenter's Bench, 7-bay Cart and Wagon Lodge, 2 single Cart Lodges with Tank Roof, large cemented Granary and Corn Store, spacious Cart Lodge and Manure Shed, capital Oast House with cemented floors, having 3 20ft. Kilns and large Cooling Room. Enclosed by these buildings are 2 large Yards and a

WELL-SHELTERED STOCK YARD,

with Covered Shed and Piggeries, whilst at the rear on the opposite side of the Right-of-way is the

EXTENSIVE STACK YARD.

Part of the sale particulars for Ditton Court Farm in May 1914

With the death of the rector, his Ditton Place estate of 28 acres was put up for sale. It was described as 'a comfortable family residence with seven bedrooms, schoolroom and two servant's bedrooms, stable, harness room, and coach house'. There was an entrance lodge on the London Road and a large oast house. The 'well timbered park' extended to Bradbourne Lane. It was purchased by William Dooner a retired army colonel and former Mayor of Rochester. Although a magistrate and a well respected lecturer on military strategy, his kindly nature was shown by a number of requests to the Parish Council to provide a seat at Ditton Corner, as 'this would be a boon to parishioners who might wish to rest here'. He and his wife were also benevolent supporters of the village school.

The interior of St Peter's Church around 1910. The east window was a memorial to John Stratton

The early years of the 20th century witnessed a rapid increase in motor traffic. Many traction engines stopped to fill up with water by the stream at Ditton Place Farm and caused considerable damage to the road surface. Damage was also done to New Road by steam wagons bringing stone from the quarry at Kiln Barn to a wharf on the River Medway. The Motor Car Act of 1903 encouraged the erection of road signs, but when one was put up at Ditton Corner in 1903, the Parish Council thought that 'it was an obstruction and dangerous to the public'. The presence of the main London Road through Ditton would prove to be an increasing problem throughout the 20th century until the construction of the M20 in 1969. The nuisance and noise created by motor traffic in Edwardian England was expressed by a petition by ten thousand so-called cottage women to the Queen. Even then 'motor cars have made our lives a misery. Our children are always in danger, our things ruined by dust, our rest is spoiled by noise at night. It would be a good thing if they could be made to go slow though our villages. We are only poor people, and the great majority of those

PARISH COUNCIL ELECTION.

NOTICE OF POLL.

ELECTION OF PARISH COUNCILLORS

FOR THE

PARISH OF DITTON

FOR THE YEAR 1913.

Names of Candidates (Surnames first).	Place of Abode.	Description.	Names of Proposer (Surname first.)
Carman, John	Belmont, Ditton	Farmer	Packham, Henry
Chantler, Peter	3 Gordon Terrace, Ditton	Labourer	Stammers, Frederick Deighton
Crittenden, William Musgrove	Bell Lane, Ditton	Builder	Stammers, Frederick Deighton
Mitchell, William Gordon	Near Cascade, Ditton	Groom-Gardener	Thorpe, William
Neve, George	Ditton Farm Cottages, Ditton	Groom-Gardener	Jenner, William James
Packham, Henry	Millhall Mill, Ditton	Miller	Williams, Daniel
Palmer, Albert	Bell Lane, Ditton	Insurance Agent	Sands, Chas. Henry
Sands, Charles Henry	Bright's Cottages, Ditton	Insurance Agent	Palmer, Albert
Scott, Thomas	Ditton Court, Ditton	Farmer	Smart, George
Smart, Alfred John	Ditton Court Farm, Ditton	Engineer	Waterman, L.
Stammers, Frederick Deighton	The Rectory, Ditton	Clerk in Holy Orders	Sands, Chas. Henry
Waterman, Leslie	Ivy Cottage, Ditton	Engineer	Smart, George
Williams, Daniel	Sunnyside, Ditton	Parish Clerk	Jenner, William James

4.—The Poll for the Parish will be taken at **THE** SCHOOL, DITTON.

5.—The Poll will be taken by ballot, and the colour of the ordinary ballot pape will be white.

Dated this 28th day of May, 1913,

FREDK. J.

A notice for a Parish Council election in 1913

who use motor-cars take no notice of us.' The Parish Council discussed the establishment of a speed limit through the village, but little was done by the County Council until 1920 when 8mph signs were erected at the narrow road between Cobdown and Ditton Place Farms. Eventually in 1927 the Kent County Council initiated a road widening scheme and this led to the demolition of the large six kiln oasthouse of Ditton Place Farm, the Ditton Place thatched lodge house, and Ivy House, formerly a public house. The road level was also raised, leading to the loss of a spectacular cascade. There is no recorded picture of any of these buildings.

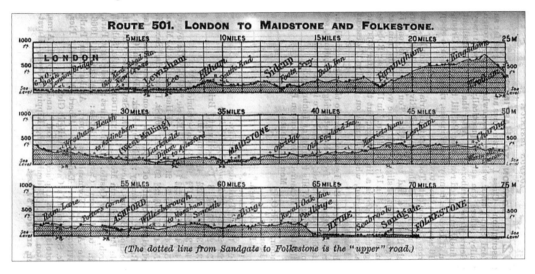

A contour map of the London to Folkestone road passing through Ditton. This enabled drivers, in the early 1920s, to avoid steep hills and to plan likely fuel consumption! (Inglis, 1923) – see page 74 for a 1675 version.

After the beginning of the First World War and the declaration of British involvement on August 4th 1914, the Parish Council took the first steps to prepare for a possible German invasion. At a meeting a few days later in August they recorded: 'The European war is now raging; to select District Police and Special Constables whose duties would be to watch and protect roads, railways and bridges, telephone and telegraph wires and poles and generally assist in maintaining the public peace.' A circular from Lord Harris, the Lord Lieutenant, 'explaining the duties of civilians in event of any landing of enemy troops, was carefully read and the contents noted'. The scouts were also enlisted in these tasks, as the School Log Book for August 1914 as 'Two members of the Boy Scouts absent today, to patrol the road by the telegraph poles'. With the sea victory at the Battle of Jutland in May 1916, the possibility of a German invasion receded.

In October 1914 a 'recruiting circular' was sent to the Parish Council, but a pertinent comment was recorded that 'the meagre allowance made to widows of

Larkfield before road widening in 1927

Above: The New Hythe turning with the Wealden Hall

Below: The turning for East Malling into New Road

Fernleigh House during the First World War. It had been requisitioned as a VAD (Voluntary Aid Detachment) Hospital. Built around 1890, this house was demolished in 1966

men killed on active service was a great hindrance to recruiting'. Until March 1916 all recruits were volunteers, but from that time conscription was introduced, and over a hundred young men from Ditton served during the war and inevitably, with a death rate of 250,000 men for each year of the war, and with double that number wounded, few families were untouched by physical or psychological injury or death. 22 from Ditton died in action or as a result of injuries. Colonel and Mrs Dooner lost two sons, one a Captain and another a Lieutant Colonel, and the recently widowed Mary Scott of Ditton Court, lost a son Captain John Scott M.C. Locally Fernleigh House in Ditton and Preston Hall were requisitioned for use as military convalescent hospitals. There was also a second casualty from Ditton Court. The sale of this 384-acre farm in 1914 by the executors of Thomas Scott was to Bernard Tolhust of Southend for £23,000, but soon after moving to Ditton, his son Lieutenant Bernard Tolhurst was killed in action.

BINGHAM. Bombr. JOHN GEORGE.	R.F.A.	PEARSON. Rifleman CHARLES E..	4th Battn. R.B.
BLUNDELL. Pte. REGINALD V..	R.W.K. Regt.	PULLEN. Gunner ALFRED C..	R.F.A.
BROWN. Gunner THOMAS.	R.F.A.	READ. Pte. WILLIAM A..	R.W.K. Regt.
DOONER. Capt. A.E.C.T..	R.W.Fusrs.	SCOTT. Capt. JOHN J.. M.C.	R.W.K. Regt.
DOONER. Lieut.Col. JOHN G..	R.F.A.	STANDING. Stoker GEORGE WILLIAM.	R.N..H.M.S. Pathfinder.
HICKS. Pte. JAMES MATTHEW.	1st. Battn. R.W.S. Regl.	STEVENS. Pte. OWEN.	R.A.M.C.
LUCAS. Pte. FREDERICK C..	27 Labour Coy.	TOLHURST. Lieut. BERNARD J..	D.of Well. Att⁴ R.A.E
MARTIN. Pte. ROBERT.	R.W.K. Regt.	TRODD. Pte. JAMES,	S.F.
MAY. Pte. ARTHUR.	167 Labour Coy.	WALTER. Gunner. EDMUND C..	R.F.A.
PALMER. Pte. AUBREY A.K..	R.M.L.I.	WILLIAMSON. Guardsman SIDNEY.	G.G.
BROOMFIELD. Corp P.T. R.War⁵ Regt		CHAPMAN. Corp W.	Mio˟ Regt

The Ditton War Memorial. The names of those killed in the 1914-1918 War
THEIR NAME LIVETH FOR EVERMORE

Apart from personal family involvement in wartime action, residents of Ditton would have been aware of increased rail traffic with the passage of hundreds of troop trains to the Kent ports, and military traffic on the London Road. A Special Constable was stationed on points duty at Ditton Corner on winter evenings, and he was provided with a box shelter by Mr Tolhurst. Householders were encouraged to grow more crops by the Board of Agriculture, and to form War Food Societies. In 1917, 60 cwt of seed potatoes were provided for Ditton gardeners. 1916 had been a bad year for harvests, and German submarines were having a significant effect on British merchant shipping.

The unveiling of the War Memorial on 26th September, 1920. Notice the absence of houses between Ditton Corner towards Preston Hall.

With the end of the war in November 1918, discussion took place within the Parish Council and village for the provision of an appropriate war memorial. Mr Tolhurst would give land at Ditton Corner for two cottages for 'two maimed soldiers or St Dunstan's to live rent free'. Other ideas from the village included a recreation ground, a drinking fountain or a German gun mounted on granite which had been offered to Colonel Dooner. In the end Mr Tolhurst, a Roman Catholic, offered a memorial consisting of a crucifix within protecting walls and roof with the names of those who had died. This was to be designed by the eminent architect Sir Giles Gilbert Scott, the designer among other things of the red phone box and Liverpool Anglican Cathedral, and grandson of the restorer of Ditton Church in 1859. This memorial did not have universal approval, in particular from the rector Frederick Stammers. However the project went ahead, and the memorial was unveiled by General Archibald Murray with a dedication by the Bishop of Rochester on 26th September 1920.

In the years of the First World War and in the following decade, the village school had approximately one hundred pupils on the roll each year. As an example, the year 1920 was divided into three classes:

Class I, 28 pupils, teacher Mr Bartholomew
Class II, 38 pupils, teacher, Mr Bartholomew
Class III, (infants) 31, teacher, Miss Bugler

The Headteacher, Frank Bartholomew, and his class in 1913

This was a settled period for the school as the teachers generally stayed for a long time. Charlotte Neath who came to the school in 1876 as a certified teacher was acting head for a while until the arrival of Frank Bartholomew in 1891. Miss Neath took charge of the infants class until she retired in 1916. When she died in 1918 the school log book recorded 'school closed, the burial of Miss Charlotte Neath who for forty years to Easter 1916 laboured in these schools'. Mr Bartholomew remained as a greatly respected head for 32 years, retiring in 1923. Both of these teachers taught two generations of many Ditton families, and for most who went no further in education than school, leaving at the age of 14 to employment, they were highly influential. All children from this era became familiar with a ditty that was sung as the children, arranged in class lines, marched into their classes at the beginning of the day:

We go to our places

With clean hands and faces,

And pay great attention to all we are told,

Or else we shall never

Be happy or clever,

For learning is better than silver or gold.

In contrast, the comments about Robert Sweet a new boy in 1918, left much to be desired: 'a boy of 12 years, who can do nothing and apparently wishes to do less'.

The rules for Ditton School Lbrary

Mr Bartholomew encouraged private reading among his pupils, and founded a school lending library. This had over three hundred volumes, and the precise rules for library membership were set out in the front of each book. He also encouraged an interest in the natural world, and with the nearby farms, fields, woods and stream he could put into practice a circular from the Board of Education:

'The teacher should take the children out of doors for short walks at the various seasons of the year, and give simple lessons on the spot about animals in the fields and farmyards, about ploughing and sowing, about fruit trees and forest trees, about birds, insects and flowers. In this way, children who are brought up in village schools will learn to understand what they see around them.'

Wheat in Stook, a picture from Nature Knowledge Readers, *a book that was used in Ditton School from 1905 to 1945. This would have been a familiar scene in Ditton during these years. Harvesting with a reaper and binder was practised at Park Farm, Bradbourne, until the 1950s.*

Before the war the Malling Rural District Council was following up a directive from the Local Government Board to build cottages within the parish. At the end of the war a piece of ground between Sunnyside and Rose Cottage (now the Rectory) was identified and six houses in three pairs were built there in 1920, the first in Ditton for around thirty years. In the years before and after the war the Parish Council, for many years under the chairmanship of the Rev'd Frederick Stammers (Rector from 1909 to 1929), expended considerable effort in providing allotments and a recreation ground for the village. Although the parish had once owned one and a half acres of allotment land at Ditton Common, this was at almost two miles' distance from most potential users and was sold to Mr May of Hermitage Farm in 1913. When the 22 acres of Ditton Common had been enclosed and sold in 1859 the value of the land, according to the rueful comments of the Parish Council in 1920 'was divided among those who had plenty and left one and a half acres which they called Ditton Poor Allotments'. Both of these problems were solved when local estates were sold and broken up. In 1924 the Larkfield estate of Samuel Lee Smith was put up for sale after his death. This consisted of Larkfield Hall, with parkland, farm and extensive stabling, and a significant portion of Ditton parish, including Fernleigh, and Cobdown House, together with Cobdown and Borough Court Farms. Samuel Lee Smith had resisted all attempts by the Parish Council in his lifetime to request him to sell a piece of land for allotments; he also proved to be an uncooperative landowner. The Parish Council was now able to purchase a plot of land near Lone Barn in Bell Lane as well as acquiring the use of additional land in Station Road for the use of 44 allotment holders. Colonel Dooner of Ditton Place died in 1926, and this estate was put up for sale a year or two later. The Parish Council was able to purchase four acres of orchard, and after two hundred fruit trees had been cleared the first village recreation ground was created. This was a great boon to the village, and was soon used for the annual village summer fetes, by the village football team and for Royal celebrations in the mid-1930s. On some Sunday evenings a local band would play here. The condition of the ground was maintained according to the Parish Council Minutes of 1930 'by use of the Larkfield Cricket Club roller and for Mr B. Carman's horse and man for 20 hours rolling per annum'.

Almost all of the parish of Ditton changed hands in the 1920s, a decade of considerable national and international economic uncertainty. The sale of Ditton Place, Fernleigh and Cobdown with associated farms mentioned already, had been preceded by the sale of the Preston Hall estate again, including Holt Wood in 1920, and in 1926 the large Ditton Court estate including Kiln Barn Farm was also sold when it was described as 'The important and famous agricultural estate'. In 1924, Cobdown and Borough Court Farms had been purchased by Mr C.B. Mercer of Broadwater, East Malling, but within two years these and the whole Broadwater estate of 970 acres was sold again. These major land changes opened the way for extensive house building in the parish between the late 1920s and the beginning of the Second World War. This will be discussed in detail later; however of more importance to the whole character of the community was the purchase of Borough Court and Cobdown Farms by the papermakers Albert E. Reed and Company Ltd.

Reeds first appear in Ditton Parish Council Minutes in 1920 in connection with requests to divert or to close footpaths. From 1917, they had been purchasing land in the vicinity of New Hythe, much of which was within the Ditton border. The founder of the company, Albert Edwin Reed was born in Cullompton, Devon in 1846, and from a lowly position as a clerk in a small paper mill in Somerset he developed an expertise in paper making, and eventually in 1894 purchased a mill at Tovil. Another purchase, Bridge Mill in Tovil, followed in 1903. With an increasing national requirement for newsprint paper, the only form of mass communication in the era before the BBC, Reeds saw the potential of the land between the River Medway and the railway at New Hythe. The river provided a convenient route for the shipment of wood pulp and china clay, and the railway with its sidings was ideal for the import in of coal and the export of paper. Pure clean water in large amounts, essential for all papermaking, was provided by the Ditton Stream which, after powering Mill Hall Mill, had discharged into the

Two street scenes in Ditton around 1920

Above: New Road

Below: Bell Lane

River Medway. Thus within one hundred years of this mill ceasing to produce handmade paper, it was owned by one of the largest paper makers within Britain.

Fancy dress at the celebration of the Silver Jubilee of George V in 1935 on the Recreation Ground

With the parallel demise of brick and cement manufacture in Burham and Wouldham, there was a large potential labour force in these and other villages including Aylesford, Ditton and East Malling, where the work of two small paper mills was coming to an end. Just over the Ditton border in Station Road a group of houses, Twelve Acres, was built for managerial staff. With the success of this major commercial venture, expansion soon took place on the south side of the railway line in the early 1930s to produce a vast industrial complex by now generally known as Aylesford Paper Mills, although a major portion was within the Ditton parish, dominated by three huge chimneys and a water tower. The land and buildings of the erstwhile Borough Court Farm were gradually demolished or allowed to fall down. As late as 1938 slates falling from the old oast house were a danger to walkers on the Bell Lane to New Hythe footpath. When this farm was sold in 1926 it was described as 'an ancient brick and tile farmhouse with stabling, a three kiln oast, with cattle and cart sheds and piggeries'. Unfortunately no effort was made to preserve any of the historic building many hundreds of years old, and there is no visual record of its structure. The Aylesford Paper Mills greatly encouraged sport among their employees, and a sports ground with cricket pavilion and football stand was created from part of the erstwhile Cobdown House park at Ditton Corner. More football pitches were created on former Borough Court farm land.

Part of Albert E. Reed's paper mill showing the East Mill with stacks of pulp.
Inset Albert E. Reed, 1846- 1920

While the north end of the parish was becoming dominated by paper making with Scandinavian tree pulp as its source, the south end of the parish was witnessing increasing work on fruit and fruit trees. Wye College Fruit Experiment Station, founded in 1913, purchased forty more acres of Ditton Court land in 1919, and a new laboratory building financed by the National Farmers Union was built right on the Ditton/East Malling parish border, and opened in 1921. By now the institute had become known as East Malling Research Station, and was owned by The Kent Incorporated Society for Promoting Experiments in Agriculture. Under the able guidance of Ronald Hatton, (later Sir Ronald), who was director from 1914 to 1948, outstanding work was carried out on fruit tree rootstocks and on soft fruit and hops, with a particular emphasis on breeding and pest and disease control. In 1929, only a few hundred yards from these laboratories, a new laboratory was built on a corner of New Gate field in Ditton. The Ditton Laboratory was a separate government initiative into fruit storage, and did not become part of East Malling Research Station until 1969. This large distinctive red brick building enclosed a simulated ship's hold. This could be refrigerated and the gaseous conditions could be modified, thus enabling scientists to study the optimum conditions for bringing fruit by ship from Australia and New Zealand (Clark and Clark, 1966).

The first laboratory, offices and stable buildings of East Malling Research Station built in 1913

The arrival of utility services gradually reached Ditton in the first half of the 20th century. A piped water supply provided by the Mid Kent Water Company from Snodland was available in most central areas of the parish by around 1920. Piped gas was available in the London Road, New Road and Bell Lane from 1912 when gas street lights were introduced. Attempts by the Parish Council to obtain an electricity supply for the village in the early 1920s failed. An approach to the Maidstone Corporation in 1923 elicited this reply: 'from a commercial point of view, a supply of electrical energy to Ditton is absolutely hopeless at this point in time'. The newly opened Reed's paper mill generated their own electricity, and Mr Tolhurst of Ditton Court Farm installed a water powered

Sir Ronald Hatton, FRS (1886-1965), the Director of East Malling Research Station from 1914-1948

turbine in the erstwhile Church Mill (which had ceased to be used for grinding in 1890), in the early 1920s. Electricity was provided for Ditton Court and Farm, Mill House and a number of cottages within the vicinity of the stream and Green. This so-called 'power house' operated until the coming of mains electricity in 1930. At the same time a hydraulic ram pump was installed on the mill waterfall to pump water to a large storage tank at Palmer's Rough field.

The disposal of waste from earth closets, buckets and cesspools was a constant point of discussion at Parish Council meetings in association with the District Council. This problem was largely solved in the early 1930s for many parts of the village apart from The Stream, Bradbourne Lane, and Station Road and outlying parts which would have required an additional pumping station, by the construction of a sewerage system with a works at the bottom of Bell Lane. With the completion of this project and with the increased availability of land, extensive house building followed. Malling Rural District Council had been hoping to build some 'cottages' in Ditton, and between 1931-2, 26 were built on the east side of New Road. Whereas there had been no houses between Ditton Corner and Preston Hall, from around 1929 a ribbon development of houses almost completely linked these two places. Also in the erstwhile Preston Hall estate, houses were built in Station road to link with the Twelve Acres Estate. In parts of

Holt Wood some superior houses were built with 'old oak, old bricks, old tiles, everything in keeping with the architecture of Tudor days.' These houses were laid out more in the style of a Garden City, with generously wide roads and with limited tree felling. Land from the former Ditton Place estate between Ditton Corner and Bradbourne Lane was developed, as well as the former park land in Bradbourne Lane from the Walnut Tree to The Stream. More houses were built on the west side of Bell Lane, formerly part of the Fernleigh Estate. Totally new roads were constructed in a number of places at this time, including the crescent of Fernleigh Rise which was incomplete at the commencement of the Second world War. A continuation of 'the opening,' called initially Orchard Valley was subsequently called Orchard Grove.

Plans for a large estate to the east of New Road along what is now Woodlands Road, the the Ditton Park Estate, amounted to only four houses at the commencement of the war. Unlike most development today where gardens are often described as 'low maintenance,' all houses then had a decent sized garden, quite sufficient to give an average family a lawn with flower garden, and a portion for vegetables for partial self sufficiency and a place for play and relaxation. Very few had garages as car ownership

PHONE: AYLESFORD 7147

A. SMITH & CO.
(MAIDSTONE) LTD.

HOLT WOOD
● AYLESFORD

Builders and Contractors

● Houses of Tudor design are being built on this estate, prices from £1,000 freehold

● No Road Charges

All Services

Mortgages Arranged

Regular Bus service to London and Maidstone

● *For full details of this unique Estate see page 8*

An advertisement in 1932 for new houses in Holt Wood.

was relatively limited although rear driveways were provided to houses on the London Road by Downderry Way off Bradbourne Lane and also for Orchard Place. Many of the new residents would work in the expanding paper mills and access to work was by walking or bicycle. For those travelling by bus to Maidstone, the Maidstone and District Bus company provided a wood shelter at Ditton Corner in 1928. The implementation of the 1934 Road Traffic Act enabled a 30 mph limit to be introduced through the village as well as a Belisha crossing at Ditton Corner in 1935.

In the 1930s an old man with his eyes shaded, and wearing a black cloak, was sometimes seen walking around Bradbourne Lane. This was Sir John Ramskill Twisden, the 12th and last baronet of a family line at Bradbourne House that stretched back to the mid 17th century. He had been born at Bradbourne House in 1856 and died there in November 1937. Although a solicitor by training, he spent much of his life recording and researching his family history. Through his efforts the baronetcy was rescued from abeyance, and his father claimed the title of 11th baronet, a title that John Ramskill inherited in 1914. His large and scholarly book *The Family of Twysden and Twisden* was completed after his death and published in 1939. A *Kent Messenger* newspaper article said:

'... he was the last of the squires of the old school. He would have nothing altered. The house had no gas or electricity and no water supply other than a well. The family went to bed with candles and slept in four-poster beds which had been aired with warming pans.'

His family had been inextricably involved with the history of Ditton for nearly three hundred years, and with his demise the beautiful park, lake and house of Bradbourne was vulnerable to speculative builders. Early in 1938 the East Malling Research Station purchased the house and grounds of two hundred acres. The house became the main office of the Research Station, the grounds and Bradbourne Farm became additional research plantations, and the parkland and lake were restored and maintained. The family portraits were left variously to the

Sir John Ramskill Twisden (1856-1937), the 12th and last Baronet of Bradbourne, painted in 1925 by Janet Brennand

Kent Archaeological Society and the National Portrait Gallery, but through an arrangement with the Research Station they were allowed to remain in the house, where they still grace the walls.

With the increase in motor traffic in the 1920s and '30s many garages were opened on the A20. There were five on the two miles between Ditton Corner and Leybourne. On the corner of Bradbourne Lane (now a Kia garage), was Ditton Service Station, and on the site of the former Ditton Place Farm, a garage linked to a civil engineering company based in Ditton Place, called SEECO (South Eastern Engineering Company). The limitation of public facilities on the road is highlighted by a complaint to the Parish Council in 1937 from residents of Holt Wood that 'motor coach parties have been using their front gardens as public conveniences'. Gradually all roads were being tar-macadamised, and this led to an expansion of stone extraction at the Kiln Barn quarry, which was provided with a railway siding, having previously used a wharf on the River Medway. In 1932, Mr Bennett of Ditton Court began quarrying operations in fields formerly known as Upper and Lower Four Acres. In addition to stone quarrying, with an extensive miniature rail system, there was a large tarring plant for the production of complete tarmac on the site.

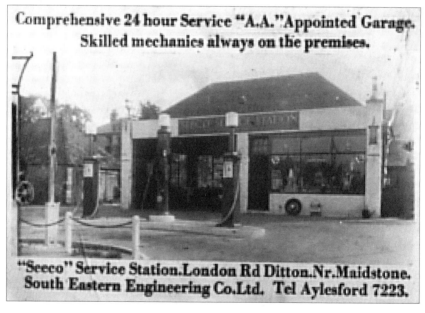

The garage and filling station of SEECO (South East Engineering Company) on the London Road near Ditton Place. In the background to left is the old stable of Ivy House (demolished in 1927). This picture was on a matchbox!

In the mid-1930s Britain was in a state of increased anxiety about a military threat from Germany. If there was to be another conflict, it would be very different from a mostly land based World War One. Now no civilian area would be free from possible air bombardment with a real possibility of the use of poison gas. As early as August 1936 Ditton Parish Council had received a government circular regarding Air Raid Precaution (ARP) and each parish was requested to nominate Head Wardens. For Ditton these were Harry Beddow, a coal merchant who lived on the London Road, and a Major Wood of The Old Mill House. A survey of the parish at that time revealed that with a population of 1236, there were 70 children under four years-old, 200 aged between 4 and 14, and 966 over 14. 162 people were prepared to serve as follows:

Street Wardens	47
First Aid	26
Firemen	22
Rescue Party	21
Transport	46

Throughout 1938 all residents were issued with gas masks (respirators), and most families possessed a hand-operated Stirrup Pump for extinguishing small fires. There was also much activity in gardens to construct underground shelters. In Bradbourne Lane, for example, there were about six shelters for 30 houses. Many homes had Morrison Shelters made from metal plate and thick wire mesh, which could be erected within a room, but made excellent chicken runs when the war ended! Window panes were covered with brown sticky tape to prevent injury through shattering. With the declaration of war on September 3rd 1939, Special Constables and ARP Wardens rigorously enforced a blackout. A signal that an invasion might be imminent would be given by a siren call from Reed's paper mill, and Barming Asylum (Oakwood Hospital). The anxiety and tension of all people at this time was shown in West Malling a few days before the declaration of war, when a fire siren caused panic among hundreds of people! Just after the outbreak of war in September, Ditton along with all parishes, welcomed hundreds of evacuees from London. In the Malling Rural District over seven thousand had to be accommodated.

Whereas the role of the ARP was predominantly concerned with protection from air raids, a new National initiative in May 1940 was for the creation of the Home Guard of Local Defence Volunteers (L.D.V.). This also stood for the 'Look, Duck and Vanish Brigade'! Any men between the ages of 16 and 65 could serve, and they would, like Dad's Army, be provided with a uniform, and some basic military training. In Ditton there was a platoon of at least 36 men who served under Captain Bennett of Ditton Court Farm. Their headquarters was in the Ditton Laboratory in Kiln Barn Road, where perhaps unknown to them, secret work was taking place in what was then the largest cold stores in England on the de-icing of aircraft wings and barrage balloons. Some of those who volunteered had lost fathers or brothers in the First World War, while some who had served in that war assisted in their training.

Ditton adjoined the Medway Defence Line, which in the likely event of a German invasion was important in strategic defence. The nearby quarry, fields and woods provided a perfect training ground. Meanwhile, at the school, a brick and concrete air raid shelter was erected on the Ditton Green side of the playground. Around the village concrete pill boxes were also erected at strategic points. On the London Road one was disguised behind a large advertising hoarding near Grand View, another on the road edge in New Road, and another within the grounds of The Old Mill House overlooking the stream ford. There were also some dragons-teeth tank traps at Ditton Corner and by the Stream Cottages.

Ditton Home Guard at Ditton Laboratory in 1940. In the centre front is Captain Bennett of Ditton Court Farm. The civilians are back left Sidney Smith, lower left Alfred Gunner, and right Doug Blundell

The personal impact of the war was soon felt in everyday life as food and clothes rationing was introduced. For those with cars, motoring was now very limited due to petrol rationing. Road signs were removed into store, and many iron railings and gates removed to be reborn as bombs and shells. In June 1940 a collection of waste metal and scrap iron around the village raised over £30 for a Red Cross Fund. In October 1940 there was a collection for the Spitfire Fund. At the outbreak of war, Mr Bennett of Ditton Court Farm immediately offered a piece of farmland in New Road as an additional space for 76 allotments. In

Stream Cottages in 1942 showing the Dragon's Teeth tank traps on the side of Stream Lane

Part of a painting entitled A 1944 Pastoral-Land Girls Pruning at East Malling, *(Research Station) by the war artist Evelyn Mary Dunbar (1906-1960). The original is in the Manchester City Art Gallery.*

his letter to the Parish Council he wrote, 'let it be said that Ditton was the first village in Kent to do something useful and practical. It is now essential to divert the minds obsessed with concerns of safety to things useful and practical'. These allotments were all taken up as the nation as a whole was encouraged to DIG FOR VICTORY. In addition many lawns and flower beds were converted into potato patches. Land Army girls were drafted in to work at Ditton Court Farm and at the Research Station. At Ditton Laboratory considerable work was in hand to improve long term potato storage, and part of this project resulted in the development of POM, an instant potato powder which was widely used in the post-war years.

One feature that made local bombing more likely, was the presence of the nearby West Malling Airfield. From a small civilian air strip established in the 1930s, this was now being converted into a fully operational RAF fighter base. When war broke out in 1939 the base was not ready for action, thus it did not play a major role in the Battle of Britain. However German observation and intelligence had identified this partially constructed base for bombing. If a German invasion was to take place, allied air fields had to be put out of operation. Residents of Ditton would have been alarmed on August 16th 1940 as 18 Dornier bombers swooped low over the village and woods, to the south and dropped 80 bombs on and around Malling airfield. Two days later there was a dive bombing attack by Junkers 87 aircraft (Brooks, 1990). Local anxiety increased in the autumn of 1940 as houses in West Malling had a number of direct hits with the loss of eight lives and with many seriously wounded. On October 31st there was a raid on Maidstone with much damage and loss of life in the Mill Street area. Ditton air raid wardens and constables were kept busy during this period, extinguishing incendiary bombs that fell at a number of places, including Kiln Barn. The front gardens of two houses on the London Road towards the Bradbourne Lane turn had their front gardens blown away, but in no case was there loss of life or injury.

Conscription for those up to the age of 41 was introduced in September 1939. As the war years proceeded many men from the village were called up, and unlike the previous war they might be drafted far away from Europe, with the declaration of war on Japan in December 1941. One Ditton resident, Len Mace of New Road, was, by early 1942, a prisoner of war in Stalag XXA. As the war years passed the tide gradually turned and the possibility of a German invasion receded. No more pill boxes were constructed, and by September 1944 the Home Guard was advised to disband. However major preparations had been in hand for some time for the D-Day landing on the beaches of France. With the Americans now fully involved in this European conflict, the London Road in early 1944 saw the passage of large convoys of American lorries and tank carriers. The troops generously handed fruit sweet bars and chewing gum to local children growing up in a world with little luxury food. The ford of Ditton Stream was used almost daily by army lorries, motor bikes and Bren-gun carriers, whose occupants were only too pleased to offer rides and sometimes gifts. With massive armament movements heading toward the coast, sometimes a local field would be taken over as a camp stopping point, with field kitchens. They vanished as quickly as they had come.

In June 1944 the last throw of German endeavour began. During a night spent in a Morrison Shelter, occupants were amazed by an unusual sound like flying motorbikes! Daylight revealed the distinctive sight of the V1 Doodlebug – a cross-shaped, unmanned, jet-driven, flying bomb. Spitfires now based at West Malling could be seen attempting to shoot these down to fall in less populated areas, or if their engines cut out, a crash to earth would be imminent. The serious damage these weapons could inflict was shown in nearby Snodland in August 1944 when one crashed on three houses in Malling Road, killing 12 people and seriously injuring 15 others. One or two of these fell in Ditton and nearby, but there were no casualties. Childhood images of this time include the recollection of a wrecked Halifax bomber in the road near West Malling Station, houses at Leybourne with fronts totally removed by bomb blast, and Doodlebug bomb craters in a field near Twelve Acres in Station Road.

Soon the war came to end with a Victory in Europe (VE) celebration bonfire and party on the recreation Ground on May 6th 1945, and a few months later another to celebrate the end of warfare against Japan (VJ) on 15th August. Church bells which had been silent for almost five years would ring again. Gradually life became more normal, air raid shelters would be used as play dens, but seven families in Ditton would have the loss of a member as a result of their military service. Their names would be joined with those of the former conflict on the war memorial.

Ditton War Memorial with the names of those who died as a result of the Second World War

The austerity of the war years was continued for all as in 1946 bread was rationed for the first time. By 1950 petrol rationing had been abolished, although sweet rationing remained until 1953. At this time Ditton had four shops that could supply some basic domestic needs; Grice in New Road, Whale in Cascade Villas, Starr in Bell Lane and Blundell at the bottom of Bell Lane. Meat could be obtained from Harry Relf who had a base in a stable off New Road. Within the village milk deliveries were available from the Gate House Dairy at the rear of Orchard Place. Shoe repairs were available by Thomas Friend in Bell Lane, and fish from Charles Swinbourne at Belmont on the London Road. Nearby Larkfield was by contrast a commercial metropolis within a short walking distance as it had a Post Office, two grocers, a butcher's shop, a bakery, a draper with shoes, a paper and sweet shop, cycle shop, hairdresser for men and a blacksmith's forge. Throughout the day vans were constantly around the village delivering bread from East Malling, Maidstone and Aylesford. Meat also came from East Malling and milk from West Malling and Aylesford. The most unique delivery was that of milk provided by Johnson's Dairy of Aylesford. This was a milk cart drawn by a horse which walked through the stream ford, and milk was still ladled from a churn.

The Maidstone and District Omnibus Company provided a regular service through the day to Maidstone every 15 minutes or so, with buses in the opposite direction passing to East and West Malling and on to either Sevenoaks, Wrotham, or Gillingham via Chatham. This meant that West Malling and Maidstone became the most important commercial destinations, whereas the lack of any public transport to Aylesford limited a commercial link in this direction, although many in the village consulted an Aylesford doctor. The lack of a post office in the village had been a cause of concern to the Parish Council since 1926. Following the introduction of old age pensions for all in 1925, the Council thought that it was too long a distance for elderly residents to walk to the far end of Larkfield to collect these. Requests made to the Post Office not only in 1926, 1932 and 1938 always elicited a negative response, although a room for use had been offered. The village had to wait until the 1950s for its own post office.

Local employment continued to be dominated by Reed's Paper Mill and associated industries, which now included Medway Corrugated Cases, Medway Paper sacks and Brookgate Industries. Near the site of the former Borough Court Farm, Holpolast, a resinous boarding, was manufactured. By now this industrial complex was over five hundred acres in extent, and employed around five thousand people in a 24-hour system of three 8 hour shifts. For all Ditton residents, each day was punctuated by a siren sounding at the change of shifts. It is estimated that well over 50% of the male working population of Ditton was now employed with this organisation. The remaining farm land of Borough Court and Cobdown Farms, together with the purchase of Cobdown House and parkland enabled Reed's and associated companies to lay out extensive sports fields. This company had owned Mill Hall Mill since the early 1920s when commercial flour production ceased. Around the end of the Second World War the old timber and

J. & E. FALCUS BUILDERS AND DECORATORS Repairs Promptly Executed 2 ORCHARD PLACE DITTON, MAIDSTONE, Kent	**H. HARRIS** 1 Ditton Park Estate PRIVATE HIRE WEDDINGS PARTIES — ETC. — AYLESFORD 7327
C. SWINBOURNE London Road, Ditton ◆ FRESH FISH DAILY ◆ Fried Fish — Afternoons and Evenings 'Phone — AYLESFORD 7140	**GATE HOUSE DAIRY** THE MISSES HUMPHREYS & HITCHCOCK PROPRIETORS **DITTON** **LARKFIELD**
STARR BROS. *Retail Grocers and Sundriesmen* **LONDON ROAD AND BELL LANE, DITTON, MAIDSTONE**	**DITTON SERVICE STATION** W. H. SQUIRES GARAGE REPAIRS PRIVATE HIRE AYLESFORD 7143
DRAPERY, BABY LINEN AND WOOLS ✶ **R. F. HUME** LONDON ROAD DITTON	**R. RELF** NEW ROAD, DITTON *GROCER PROVISION MERCHANT*

*Some shops and businesses in Ditton as advertised in the Church Magazine
in May 1947*

brick mill house and most of the mill building was demolished. Unfortunately no photographic record of this mill was made. The 14 feet diameter and six feet wide waterwheel, manufactured and installed by 'W. Weeks Maidstone 1887' was left in place. Thus ended the life and presence of a water mill which had been first recorded and described 883 years before, in 1086, in the Manor of Sifleton as 'One mill worth 10 shillings'. Although Cobdown Farm had been run as a profitable commercial enterprise through the 1920s and 30s, and included a good acreage of hops, the requisition of its land for sports fields made the farm buildings redundant. An ancient barn, which was described in 1926 as 'a brick weatherboard and thatched barn', probably dating from the Twisden's ownership from the 17th or 18th century, was demolished. The four kiln mid-Victorian oast house fared better. This was restored, and the cooling room floor was removed to create a baronial-style dining room with a gallery. This was to be a clubhouse for Reed employees, and was named after an influential Managing Director as The Clifford Sheldon Club House. With the loss of four other sets of oast houses within the village in the last eighty or so years, it is the only tangible reminder of erstwhile hop production in Ditton.

Cobdown Farm Oasthouse in 1935. Bringing in the full hop pokes for drying. The wagon is a traditional cream or stone coloured Kentish model. The hop pokes are embellished with the name of the farmer H.A. BELLINGHAM, Maidstone. Henry Bellingham lived at Gatland Farm, Tonbridge Road, Maidstone.

Farming continued however at Ditton Court Farm, centred on the fine range of stone and slate farm buildings just off Ditton Green. Fifteen to twenty men,

*Interior of the former Cobdown Farm oasthouse in 1950 after conversion
into the Clifford Sheldon Club House by the Reed Paper Group*

mostly living in nearby farm cottages were employed on the farm. Now, in
addition to the main crops of hops and fruit the farm had a fine herd of pedigree
Guernsey cows. A new house for the cowman had been built on the edge of The
Green near the church. The highlight of the farm year was hop picking in late
August and early September. On this farm only local labour was employed. A
row of 14 hopper huts at Kiln Barn still remained from the time when pickers
came from London, but these had not been used for many years. Hop gardens had
permanent poles and wires and the hop bines were grown up strings arranged
in an umbrella formation. Each family bin, or two families with half bins, was
allocated a row. A hop bine was pulled down and the hops were picked by hand
into the sacking bins. Twice each day the measurer and his team with bookie and
binman came round to record the amount picked.

Family groups of hop pickers

Above: The early 20th century (circa 1910) with hops still grown on poles

Below: Pickers at East Malling Research Station in the 1940s

In the late 1940s, in the time of Farmer Bennett, Jack was the measurer, using his old hop-blackened basket. He sweated away, calling out the number of bushels as he tipped them into a poke (hop sack) held by binman, Henry; the bookie was a retired teacher. The pokes were tied up and left for collection by Charlie who at that time had a horse drawn old Kentish wooden wagon, and were taken off to the oast house. Drying was the skilled job of his brothers Fred and Harry, assisted by Alf and Dave. The three 18-feet square kilns from the second half of the 19th century had superseded the former two kiln, circular oast that had existed near the farmhouse. Hops from the pokes were distributed about two feet deep on a horse hair covered slatted floor about two thirds of the way up the main chamber.

At this time there was a coal furnace on the floor below, often with sulphur added to improve the colour of the dried hops. The skilled hop dryer had to decide when the heat had reduced the water content of the hops from about 80% to 6% by skill and experience. He was on hand for 24 hours a day to make sure that that drying was complete. The hops were then removed from the large drying floor and then pressed firmly into a sacking hop pocket. When full, these would weigh about one and a half hundredweight, and would be embellished with the name of the farmer and the year of production. Thus for a few weeks of the year, the area around Ditton Court Farm, the church and The Green, basked in the unique and evocative aroma of drying hops. Once picking was finished and all the calculations had been made, the picker families, now almost unrecognisable in their smartness, queued at the farm office to collect their dues at a time appointed. The long hours of hard work and scratches from the bines had been worth the effort, as a new ten pound note was received with delight! (There are excellent descriptions of hop picking and associated activities in Warren, 1937 and Orwell, 1964).

Growing hop bines; a familiar Ditton sight in Kiln Barn Road (now the Kilnbarn Recreation Ground) until 1959

At this time the Ditton School playing field backed on to one of the hop gardens. In the months after the end of the war German prisoners of war, based in a camp near Well Street in East Malling, were sometimes working on the land. Friendly and happy greetings were always exchanged, and young minds were perplexed by the paradox of their quiet courtesy and the recent events of aggression and destruction. Mr Robert Toomey who had been Headmaster since 1924, delayed his retirement until the end of the war, and in 1946 was replaced by Mr Harold Goodban. Mr. Goodban's enthusiasm for sport was soon apparent in athletics, football and cricket. His particular love was cricket, but he did not live to see his grandson, Paul Downton, play cricket for England.

Due to the economic hardships of the 1920s and the restrictions of war time, the school was little changed in structure and furnishings from the Edwardian era. Classrooms were still formally arranged with wood and metal pairs of desks with ink wells and heated by coke burning stoves. Outside toilets were prone to freezing up, so schooling was cancelled for the day! However, excellent educational foundations were laid to be built on, remembered and cherished.

The senior class at Ditton School in 1948 with the headmaster, Mr Goodban
Back row from left: Peter Chapman, Tommy Gibbs, Rufus Kenchington, John
Braybrooke, Donald Brunger, Donald Martin, John Beadle, Michael Merrett, Edgar
Fullager, H.H. Goodban
Middle row: Harry Harris, Maureen Swinbourne, John Gladdish, Maureen Smissen,
Tony Humphreys, Maureen Monson, Joan Staines, Shirley Steel, Alan Dodge
Front row. Shirley Jenner, Eileen Wood, Helen Tolhurst, Eileen Beaumont, Marjorie
Warne, Pat Robbins, Cherry Price, Margaret Woodger, Florence Rich

Chapter 9

The Modern World: 1950-2011

Ditton was once all fruit orchards and hop gardens, now it is all houses and roads.

Ditton Remembered. Don Carman, 1917-2003

The years from 1900 to 1950 had witnessed a seismic shift in landownership and society in England. Two World Wars, and the massive socio-economic changes of the inter war years, led to a society that had lost the relatively unquestioned hierarchy of former times. In Ditton, this was shown in the demise of the Preston Hall estate which had owned a major part of the parish, and was, in its day, a symbol of Victorian wealth and power. Just over sixty years after the completion of a new mansion, this had become part of a hospital and re-settlement centre in the British Legion Village. Bradbourne House, for over three hundred years an influence on the history of Ditton had become the offices and library for East Malling Research Station. Nearby, Larkfield Hall was a children's home for the Steiner Foundation, and Leybourne Grange was part of a large county mental hospital, Addington Place, Fatherwell House and Trosley Towers have all been demolished. Birling Manor was badly damaged by fire in 1917 and was never rebuilt, although the Neville family still have a residence in that village, as they have done since 1435!

In Ditton the overriding influence continued to be the Reed industrial conurbation now ever larger with the arrival of Kimberley Clark to manufacture Kleenex tissues. Their playing fields were becoming more extensive with the loss of farmland, ironically now called Larklands. Cross country running was now much to the fore, and the English National Cross Country Championship took place on their grounds in 1951, with a race of seven and a quarter miles over three laps over Cobdown Hill. Some of the Aylesford Paper Mills' cross country team participated in carrying the Olympic Torch through the village on the night of 29th July 1948. Sporting facilities were complemented by social activities centred on the Jubilee Hall in New Hythe, and a Finnish-donated Sauna Bath House. In these post war years Ditton Football Club was reformed, playing home matches on the Recreation Ground, with a base for the team in the Working Men's Club in New Road (now the Kentish Quarryman). The team had outstanding success in some of these years, becoming champions of the first division of the Maidstone and District League in 1951, and in 1953 beat local rivals Eccles to win the Maidstone and District League Challenge Shield.

Ditton Football Club, winners of the Maidstone and District Charity Shield in 1953
Back row from left: Ben Banks, Eric Bale, Jack Edy, Reg Rich, Bob Capon, Ken Vinten,
Don Steel, Henry Standing
Front row: Alf (Bill) Savage, George Mount, Ernie Rayfield, John Banks, Jack Brimstead,
Ted Jarvis, Hugh Vinten, Ron Whitbread

Also revitalised in the early post-war years was the Village Fete which had been founded in 1908. This was held on the Recreation Ground on a summer Saturday, and was preceded by procession of children from the bottom of Bell Lane led by a brass band. All children were given a small sum of money to spend at the Fun Fair, and there were competitive sports, including the unique greasy pole. Penfold's Funfair included a steam driven roundabout, complete with fairground organ, and the amusements were hauled to the Recreation Ground by a large steam traction engine which also generated the electricity to light up the evening festivities.

By around 1950 house building was being resumed. Fernleigh Rise, incomplete at the commencement of war was completed, and Malling Rural District Council initiated a new phase of house building. The initial pre-war development of Ditton

A village scene in December 1950. Carol singing in the snow by members of St.Peter's Church at Stream Cottage. The rector, Philip Scott is in the centre, and the two churchwardens, Don Carman and Bernard Barber are on the right. Esther Gladdish and Nellie Summers listen at the cottage door.

The cowman's house, Ditton Court Farm, (demolished around 1965), now the site of St Peter's Court.

Park Estate to the east of New Road was now extended into what would become Woodlands Road. This followed the track of an ancient farm road across what had formerly been Ditton Place Farm land, and called in the 17th century 'Great Sheeplands' and, in the 1840s, 'Goldings Hop Garden'. The building of fifty or so houses on this land was soon followed by a northerly extension of fifty houses in Link Way and Medina Road, all on Ditton Court Farm Land.

The ownership of Ditton Court Farm had by now passed from Henry Bennett to his son-in-law Montague Thompson Coon. His entrepreneurial endeavours would soon lead to a major change in the activities of the farm. With the installation of a refrigeration plant he was able to freeze soft fruits, and a new business 'Frozen Fruits (Ditton Court)Ltd.', emerged. Soon a major part of the late Victorian farm buildings had been converted into a factory, now producing canned and frozen fruit and vegetables. The tins were all labelled with the trade name 'Peterhouse', with pictures of St Peter's Church, Ditton Court Farmhouse, and a farm building with three oast houses. In addition to this enterprise, a nursery for fruit trees continued to flourish on land that subsequently became *Nursery Road.*

By now an increasing number of local people were employed in the Ditton Court enterprises, and on some days during winter months, the cooling chamber of the oast house was converted into an impromptu cinema for employees. However, economic necessity forced a sale of the whole enterprise in 1960. Much of the remaining farmland of around 140 acres was purchased by East Malling Research Station; Ditton Court farmhouse was sold separately, and other parcels of land in Mill Orchard and Crabtree Mead were sold for building, to become the 70 houses of St Peter's Road, St Peter's Close and Wilton Drive. The canning factory continued as a working unit of an Irish company, New Forge, with the local name of 'Blue Cap Foods (Kent) Limited'. Thus within the space of fifty years each of the four major hop and fruit farms, once the backbone of Ditton's employment and economy, had ceased to exist. Mr Thompson Coon and his family moved away to farm in Northamptonshire, and his eldest daughter Caroline became notable in the 1960s as an artist and journalist, and for her work among drug addicts.

With an increase in private car ownership, employment was available over a much wider area. Long gone were the days when all walked to work in the village, or cycled nearby. Ditton, as part of the Medway Gap development, and with little conservation or Greenbelt control, now together with adjacent Larkfield and Leybourne, was vulnerable to major housing development. The sewerage system was extended in 1957 to Bradbourne Lane and The Stream, and a large new works was opened in Lower Bell Lane. The infrastructure and land were now available for extensive housing development between 1960 and 1970. These included over one hundred houses in Priory Close off Station Road, partially on a field called 'Shoulder of Mutton'.

The label from a can of Peterhouse cherries (circa 1954). The label incorporates St Peter's Church, Ditton Court Farmhouse, and the oasts of Ditton Court Farm.

Woodlands Road was now extended across arable fields to Holt Wood, where it looped around the wooded hill to emerge at Tea Pot Lane. The naming of roads as Primrose Drive, Acorn Grove, Cedar Close and Birch Crescent is a reminder of some of the flora of this erstwhile chestnut coppice wood. This new development consisted of over two hundred houses in Ditton alone. Although Holt Wood had been privately owned, it was accessible by public paths and other tracks. In centuries past it was the nearest wood for the cottagers of Ditton who would have obtained their fuel 'by hook or by crook', as well as being a children's playground. There was a longstanding Ditton tradition that villagers would visit the woods to walk or to picnic on Good Friday, a custom some maintained until the 1950s. Bank Holidays were only introduced in 1871, but before that time Christmas Day and Good Friday were the only holidays granted to most workers. A walk with family and friends to Holt Wood on Good Friday was to the agricultural labourers and families of past time, a highlight of their year. This would have been the later equivalent of a day to the sea, and it was always the day for planting potatoes! The summerhouse on the top of Holt Hill had once been a favourite meeting place for the Brassey family of Preston Hall (Sephton,1997). Unfortunately no benefactor or philanthropist was around in the 1930s and 1960s to preserve this beautifully wooded hill as a public open space. It would have been especially welcome in an increasingly urbanised environment!

Through the 1940s and '50s, Fernleigh House had been inhabited by Colonel William Ogg and his family. He had had a distinguished career in the Royal Artillery, being awarded the DSO and CMG. Like Colonel Dooner, who lived at Ditton Place forty years earlier, he was also a military strategist, and at some time lectured on Military History and tactics at Sandhurst. His son, Stuart, used the grounds as well as further plantations in Swanley to grow delphiniums and dahlias for which he was nationally famous. In summer time the fields around Fernleigh were a blaze of colour. After Colonel Ogg died in 1958 at the age of 85, the house and land were sold, and the late Victorian house demolished in 1966. Across the village boundary into Larkfield, Larkfield Hall had also been purchased for development and demolished. This new development, like that in Holt Wood, was also given tree names, the roads linking to Bell Lane being called Oak Drive, Blackthorn Drive and Chestnut Walk. Others included Hornbeam Close and most appropriately, The Ferns.

Looking across Green Field and Holt Field towards Holt Wood from St Peter's Church tower in 1961. The two early 19th century farm cottages on the right were demolished around 1965.

In the late 1960s the large Victorian Rectory in Kiln Barn Road was proving to be too large, and the grounds too extensive. A replacement was found in 1969 at Rose Cottage on The Green. The old rectory was purchased for development, but before this could take place it was gutted by fire and demolished. This rectory had had a large cherry orchard, and this name was given to the housing development on the site. The regrettable loss of the two large Victorian houses within a few years was followed by a third in 1972, Ditton Court. This was unfortunately just outside a newly created Conservation Area of Ditton Green and Stream (see below). The juxtaposition of church and manor court house had existed since

Norman times, reflecting the two ever interweaving strands of village history, the sacred and the secular. This physical link was broken in 1972 when Ditton Court was demolished, and Ditton Court Close was built. Meanwhile, the gentle presence and influence of St Peter's Church continues to be felt in the midst of an ever changing community.

At weekends and bank holidays in the late 1940s and early 1950s the Kent coast was a favoured destination for coach day trips from London. The London Road through Ditton was one of the key routes for these excursions, and traffic hold-ups were frequent. The importance of the A20 was shown by its designation as the first Trunk Road in Kent, in 1937. The passage of traffic through Maidstone was a particular problem, and much was diverted at Ditton Corner through Aylesford, Sandling, and Penenden Heath. A by-pass for Maidstone had been planned in the mid 1930s, and some land had been purchased, but further developments were inhibited by the war. Work re-commenced in 1958 and a road from near Coldharbour Lane, Preston Hall to Leeds, was opened in 1960. This did nothing to relieve the traffic through Ditton, and work on the so-called Ditton by-pass, to become the M20, was begun in 1969. This new road cut through Ditton from New Hythe Lane to Mill Hall in a journey time of about 45 seconds at 70 mph! It is hard to envisage a greater contrast between this Lower Bell Lane part of Ditton, a hundred or so years earlier and today. Here was a small, isolated farm holding then appropriately called *Lone Barn:* now there are thousands of vehicles passing every hour.

An M 20 sign located on the edge of Cobdown (compare this with the picture on page 76!)

Passing the sewage works, the motorway cut through the side of Cobdown Hill, across the pond of Mill Hall Mill, and under the Station Road near Twelve Acres and Mill Hall. The loss of the waterwheel of this mill at that time, left after the demolition of the mill in the 1940s, is poignantly expressed by Michael Fuller, the local mill historian:

'An almost perfect example of an overshot waterwheel and its pentrough were demolished to make way for the foundations of a footbridge that now spans the M20 motorway. Had the bridge been re-sited by only a few feet we could have continued to see the prime cause for the naming of this area Mill Hall. This is merely one example of the fate, which can affect the remains of so much which we profess to hold dear, but to which so little attention is paid.' (Fuller,1980)

The opening of this six and a half mile motorway in December 1971 was proudly and optimistically advertised by the contractors, Costain, under the title of 'Silent Night in Ditton', with a note that the £4.4 million project was completed four weeks ahead of schedule.

The need for a meeting and social facilities room/hall in Ditton had long been felt. Discussions within the Parish Council concerning this went back to the mid 1930s. A suggestion was made in 1935 that the village 'raise money to build a Village Institute, and the formation of cricket and football teams, regular holding of dances, whist drives and concerts, annual sports and old folks teas.' The war years prevented any further developments, but immediately war ended a 'Ditton Village Hall Memorial Committee' was set up in 1946. The raising of money as well as a suitable site proved too difficult at that time. In spite of this the Mission Hall in Bell Lane was much used by the vigorous Scout movement with its associated Cubs, Guides and Brownies. The Working Men's Club hall was used by some village activities such as DATS (Ditton Amateur Theatrical Society), while others used the large drill hall of the Territorial Army on the London Road. With the demise of Ditton Court Farm there was more land available, and so a large Community Hall, with associated playing fields was established by the Parish Council in 1974. The large hall, appropriately called Oaken Hall after Oaken Wood at Ditton Common, had accommodation for four hundred, while smaller halls were called the Acorn and Carman Rooms.

Don Carman was a village resident for his whole life, and had devoted many years to the Parish Council and Parish Church (Carman, 2003). This centre and the Kiln Barn Recreation Ground fulfilled the long felt need for community facilities, and are now used by about thirty village sporting and social activities. Around the same time Ditton Primary and Infants Schools had much needed new buildings on nearby land, but retained the original school playing areas. The earliest erstwhile Ditton Primary School buildings became the new Church Centre and the infants department, after a period as a swimming bath, was resurrected as Ditton Heritage Centre in 1996 to teach children in the style of a Victorian school. The year before, 1995, had seen the establishment of a twinning relationship with Rang-du-Fliers a small town south of Le Touquet in north east France. With the opening of the Channel Tunnel in 1994, and Eurostar train operations from Waterloo Station in 1997, High Speed trains were often seen passing through Ditton to and from France on the railway line at Kiln Barn.

The cause of heritage and conservation in the village was enhanced in 1971 by Malling Rural District Council in designating an area around Ditton Green, St Peter's Church and the Stream as an area of special architectural and historic interest. This was too late to prevent the churchyard from being hemmed in by the modern development of St Peter's Court. In 1974, after the creation of Tonbridge and Malling Council, part of the Holt Wood Estate, built in the Tudor style in the 1930s in 'an Arcadian setting with tree lined roads' was also designated as a conservation area (Miller, 1974). A few years later, the Ditton Conservation Area was extended to include part of Bradbourne Lane, the area of stream by St Peter's Road, and the old school and farm bungalows. With the closure of the quarry in Kiln Barn Road in 1984, part of the land was developed with houses in the appropriately named Ragstone Court. With the loss of so much green space over the previous 30 years, it was appropriate that 15 acres of the quarry land was obtained by the Parish Council, and in 1994 was designated as 'Ditton Quarry Nature Reserve'. With expert guidance in conservation, this area was identified as a Site for Nature Conservation in 1999, and part of it as a Local Nature Reserve by Natural England in 2006. Now over 140 wild flower species, including some orchids, 18 butterfly species and over fifty birds have been identified on the site.

The cause of architectural conservation in the village was dealt another severe blow on a night in March 1987. The recently vacated Ditton Place and Grounds, together with some of the hinterland of Bradbourne Lane was being developed for housing. The Parish Council had resisted demolition of Ditton Place, but an arsonist initiated a blaze that took nine hours to control. The largely Mid-Victorian house, the largest in the village, had incorporated part of a much earlier house of the Goldings and Brewers. What was lost among other things were described at the time as 'a magnificent staircase, a beautiful coving on the ceiling: a marble fireplace and stained glass window.' The house was not restored, but Troutbeck House with a similar footprint was built in its place, together with houses in Ditton Place and Streamside.

Although the history of Ditton over the last thousand years has been that of a small community dominated by agriculture, the emerging story of the 20th century has been that of a community in which plants and plant products still play a pivotal role. The paper industry with gigantic mills within the Ditton border has been totally dependent on plant (wood) fibres; East Malling Resarch Station, with laboratories and plantations within Ditton parish, has achieved world famous work on fruit trees and bushes; fruit and vegetable canning and freezing has been carried on at Ditton Court, as have scientific studies of fruit and vegetable storage at Ditton Laboratory, though both are now closed. In the late 1940s and '50s, the firm of Chittenden and Symonds with offices and works at Ditton Place, provided wood mosaic flooring for the Festival of Britain in 1951. An activity that goes on almost unchanged from past centuries is the growing of chestnut coppice plantations providing fencing, poles and firewood.

Ditton Laboratory, a distinctive brick building of 1929 as photographed in 2011. Future uncertain

The 1960s was a period of decline and near closure for the Reed Paper Group at Aylesford. However, increasing environmental concern and the evolution of new techniques has led to the formation of Aylesford Newsprint, a company that now produces one per cent of the world's newspaper from recycled newspapers and magazines. Around two million tonnes of newspapers and over one million tonnes of magazines are reutilised at the Aylesford site each year. One paper making machine produces newsprint paper nine metres wide at a rate to stretch from Aylesford (Ditton!) to Athens in 24 hours. It is reckoned that each wood fibre can be recycled seven or eight times.

Part of the large industrial complex of Aylesford Newsprint looking north from the edge of the M 20 at Cobdown. The large building to the left is part of the former West Mill of Albert E. Reed and Co.

East Malling Research Station had a period of considerable expansion in the twenty or so years after the war. New laboratories were built and staff numbers increased to over three hundred employees. New houses for farm workers were built in Bradbourne Lane in the late 1940s and named 'Amos Bank' after Jesse Amos, the farm and plantations manager for many years. To emphasise the importance of agriculture in the post war years, a plaque on these houses was unveiled by Tom Williams, the Minister of Agriculture, in 1947. In addition to extensive work on disease and pest control and optimal conditions for tree or bush growth and propagation, a continual new stream of varieties of apples, pears, cherries, plums, raspberries, strawberries, gooseberries, and black and red currants were released. The work of Ditton Laboratory which did ground breaking work on gaseous fruit storage was integrated into East Malling Research Station in 1969, but was subsequently moth-balled. Major changes in government funding and a restructuring of horticultural research in England in the 1980s led to the closure of a number of other research institutes, and the amalgamation of East Malling with others into the Institute for Horticultural Research. This became Horticulture Research International by amalgamation with the former government advisory service in 1990. With a continuous drop in government support for horticultural and agricultural research, the laboratories became an independent company in 2004 as East Malling Research. The original work on fruit still continues, now supplemented by a range of other investigations into biomass and novel food crops, as well as a plant clinic to identify and advise growers on pests and diseases. Significant recent work is the genetic modification of plants to produce drugs that control the HIV virus.

In the far south of the parish, coppicing of chestnut woodland is still practised as it has been for centuries. From a tree stool, shoots grow for ten or twelve years and whereas in former times the axe was used to chop these down, now it is the chainsaw. Chestnut poles, for a long time used for hop poles, are also valuable for fencing. Unfortunately, this Oaken Wood area of Ditton with its oak standard trees and valuable wildlife, is under considerable threat from quarrying. Already 74 acres around Broke Wood and the eastern edges of Oaken Wood, including the former Ditton Common which once had been a part of the village for all to use and enjoy has been destroyed by deep quarrying. A large concrete underpass has been constructed in what was a crossing of woodland tracks and the ancient earthwork of

A common sight at East Malling Research Station until around 1980. A horse drawn hoe could be used in all weathers between the nursery stock of fruit trees.

Well Wood has been destroyed. Considerable concern was expressed in 1995 about the work of bulldozers and bonfires in destroying woodland, and more plans are afoot to destroy further areas of the woodland here for stone quarrying. The anxiety felt by so many of further woodland destruction in the parish is quite justified, as these woods are one of the few places within the parish boundary where we can find quiet, be free to walk, away from traffic, and enjoy the beauty and diversity of the natural world. Woodland is an appropriate place to end this historical journey through a Kentish parish. It brings the story of Ditton full circle from the nomads who hunted in woodland here in 7,000-8,000 BC, to the woods today. It also highlights the dilemma we face in the new millennium of balancing 'progress,' involving more houses, roads and cars, against the presence of woodland and recycling to counteract global warming, and to the survival of life as we know it !

The Ditton Parish sign that was erected
at Ditton Corner in 1996

EPILOGUE

This book has attempted to show how a small Kentish parish evolved over many thousands of years. The sources available for this study have included the physical evidence of archaeology, buildings and landscape, some hand-written records from the Domesday Book to Parish Council Minutes, printed records, pictures, photographs and maps, as well as personal reminiscences and memories. It has been all the more important to record the past of Ditton, as the landscape of large parts of the parish has been overlaid by modern development. Many former fields and field boundaries as well as an ancient earth work have been obliterated. Ancient roads, tracks and pathways and have been destroyed or diverted for the convenience of landowners and developers, and historic buildings needlessly demolished, and woodlands have been destroyed by quarrying.

Looking across to Ditton Court Farm from Bradbourne Lane in 1959. Guernsey cows graze in a field soon to be built over. 1959 was the last year of farming at Ditton Court Farm, thus ending a manor/village activity that stretched back a thousand years or more to Saxon Dictune.

North of the Motorway virtually every remnant of the past has gone. Two brick arches from the 1850s under the New Hythe to Aylesford railway line which connected Borough Court Farm with its riverside meadows, and another that linked Bell Lane to Old Ead Lane and a river wharf, now cower in the midst of a vast industrial complex. Mill Hall Mill, apart from the remnants of the mill pond, is now an overgrown scrubby bank surrounded by barbed wire. On the site of the former Ditton Court Farm buildings over ninety residences have recently been built in under four acres with scant regard for the ancient right of way from Ditton Green to East Malling. It is an interesting contrast to think that in the reign of Elizabeth I an Act of Parliament required each newly built cottage to have four acres of land! This law was repealed in 1775. Whereas in 1801 Ditton was one of the most sparsely populated parishes in the area, two hundred years later it is one of the most densely populated. Ditton church alone among all medieval churches in the former Malling Rural District was excluded from books on Kent Country Churches (Syms, 1984, 1987, 1989) because it was in the author's view 'no longer a country village.'

The survival of the buildings of Cobdown Farmhouse and farm buildings are now the only reminders of the dominant role of agriculture in the parish economy. The buildings of the Stream Conservation Area, now surrounded on all sides by more and more houses, still point to a time almost a thousand years ago and the presence of a Norman Manor, with three key features of church, manor house (Ditton Court) and the manor mill. This was the hub of the small community of Dictune, with open fields stretching towards the woodlands of Holt Wood, Kiln Barn and Oaken Wood. The church building with family monuments, and the churchyard with gravestones name some who have figured in this written history. Equally important are those 'who have no memorial,' and whom we only know from the three key events of the Parish Registers.

The gentle stream still flows on, reminding us of the vital life and power that sustained this community for centuries, but now seems almost incidental to our modern society. This has been the story of a Kentish community on this stream, *Dictune*/Ditton.

> *There was a time when meadow, grove,*
> > *and stream,*
> *The earth, and every common sight,*
> > *To me did seem*
> *Apparelled in celestial light,*
> *The glory and the freshness of a dream.*
> *It is not now as it hath been of yore;-*
> > *Turn wheresoe'er I may,*
> > > *By night or day,*
> > *The things which I have seen I now can*
> > > *see no more.*

From *Intimations of Immortality from Recollection of Early Childhood.*
William Wordsworth, 1770-1850

FURTHER READING and REFERENCES

Abbreviations:
AC	Archaeologia Cantiana	
CKS	Centre for Kentish Studies (formerly Kent Archives Office)	
KAS	Kent Archaeological Society	
VCH	Victoria County History	

Further reading with information about Ditton and nearby:
Dodge, A.D., *Ditton – The Church and Parish. St Peter's, Ditton*, PCC, 1978
East Malling Trust for Horticultural Research. *Bradbourne House, East Malling, Kent*, 2006
Fielding, C.H., *Memories of Malling and its Valley; with A Fauna and Flora of Kent*
H.C.H. Oliver, West Malling, 1893
Fuller, M.J., *The Watermills of the East Malling and Wateringbury Streams*. Christine Swift, 1980
Hasted, E., *The History and Topographical Survey of the County of Kent*. Articles on Ditton, pages 455-463, and nearby parishes in Volume 4, 1798. Now available as British History on line..
Ireland, W.H., *A New Complete History of the County of Kent*. Vol. III, 1829
McNay, M., *Portrait of a Kentish Village. East Malling 827-1978*. Gollancz, 1980
Newman, J., *The Buildings of England: West Kent and the Weald*. Penguin, 1969. Ditton on page 251

Further reading with background information on Kent and Kent History
Jessup, F.W., *A History of Kent*. Phillimore, 1974
Jessup, F.W., *Kent History Illustrated*. KCC, 1966
Lawson, T and Killingray, D.(eds), *A Historical Atlas of Kent*. Phillimore, 2004
McRae, S.G. and Burnham, C.P., *The Rural Landscape of Kent*. Wye College, 1973
McRae, S.G. and Burnham, C.P., *Kent the Garden of England*. Paul Norbery, 1978
Page, W. (ed), *Victoria County History of Kent*, Vol. I, 1908: Vol. II, 1926: Vol. III, 1932

REFERENCES cited in each chapter of the text
Chapter 1: **SETTING THE SCENE** (pages 9-23)
Cecil, D., *Two Quiet Lives*. Constable, 1948
Field, J., *English Field Names; A Dictionary*. Sutton, 1989
Mills, A.D., *Dictionary of English Place Names*. Oxford, 1991
Pearce, S.C. and Greenham, D.W.P., 'A Short History of Research Station Land in the Parishes of Ditton and Aylesford.' Annual Report, page 49, East Malling Research Station, 1965

Chapter 2: **PREHISTORIC AND ROMAN HISTORY** (pages 24-29)
Clark, J.G.D., *The Mesolithic Age in Britain*. Cambridge, 1932
Evans, A.J., Late-Celtic Urn-Field at Aylesford, Kent. Archaeologia, 52, page 280, 1890
Everitt, A., *Continuity and Colonisation. The Evolution of the Kentish Settlement*. University of Leicester Press, 1986
Fielding, C. H., *Memories of Malling and its Valley*. H.C.H. Oliver, West Malling, 1893
Kelly, D.B., 'An Anglo Saxon Spearhead from Ditton'. AC, LXXVII, page 204, 1962
Page, W. (ed.), 'Ancient Village Sites. Aylesford, Preston Woods.' VCH I, page 435, 1908
Palmer, S., 'Flint Artefacts from Holt Hill, near Aylesford.' AC LXXX, page 258, 1965
Pirie, E., 'A note on a Roman Villa at East Malling.' AC, LXXI, page 208, 1957
Wacher, A., 'A note on a Roman Villa at East Malling.' AC, LXXX, page 257, 1965
Williams, J.H. (Ed), *The Archaeology of Kent To AD 800*. Boydell Press/KCC, 2007

Chapter 3: **AN ANGLO SAXON AND NORMAN COMMUNITY** (pages 30-38)
Bede. *Ecclesiastical History of the English People*. Penguin, 1980
Berg M. and Jones, H., *Norman Churches in the Canterbury Diocese*. The History Press, 2009
Everitt, A., *Continuity and Colonisation. The Evolution of Kentish Settlement*. University of Leicester Press, 1986
Gee, H. and Hardy, W.J., *Documents Illustrative of English Church History*. Macmillan, 1896
Hicks, C., *The Bayeux Tapestry*. Vintage, 2007
Livett, G.M., 'Early Norman Churches in and near the Medway Valley.' AC XX, page 137, 1893
Morris, J. (ed.), *Domesday Book, Kent*. Philimore, 1983
Oakley, A.M., *Malling Abbey, 1090-1990*. Malling Abbey, 1990
Page, E (ed.), 'Domesday Kent. Dictune and Sifltone.' VCH, III, 1932
Swanton, M.J. (ed) *The Anglo Saxon Chronicle*. Dent, 1997
Ward, G., 'The List of Saxon Churches in the Textus Roffensis.' AC XLIV, page 39, 1932
Williams, C.L.S., 'A Rental of the Manor of East Malling A.D. 1410, in A Kentish Miscellany', ed. F.Hull. Kent Records, KAS, 1979

Chapter 4: **MEDIEVAL TIMES; CHURCH AND MONASTIC INFLUENCE** (pages 39-51)

Berg, M and Jones, H., *Norman Churches in the Canterbury Diocese*. The History Press, 2009.

Braun, H., 'The Carmelite Friary of Aylesford.' AC LXII, 1950.

Calendar of Inquisitions (1362), Vol IX, Public Record Office.

Duncan, L.L., *Testamenta Cantiana. West Kent*, page 22. Hughes and Clarke,1906.

Greenstreet, J., 'Assessments in Kent for the aid to Knight the Black Prince, Anno 20 Edward III.' AC X, page 99, 1876

Harley, H.A. and Chalklin, C.W., 'The Kent Lay Subsidy of 1334/5 in Documents Illustrative of Medieval Kentish History,' ed. F.R.H. Du Boulay. Kent Records, KAS, 1964

'Inquisitiones Post Mortem.' AC. IV, page 311, 1861

Jessup, F.W., 'Calendar of Kentish Feet of Fines.' Kent Records XV, KAS, 1956

Knowles, D. and Hadcock, R. N., *Medieval Religious Houses in England and Wales*. Longman, 1971

Langland, W., *Piers the Ploughman*. (1370) Penguin, 1966

Lees, P., *Nunneries, Learning and Spirituality in late Medieval English Society. The Dominican Priory of Dartford*. The York Medieval Press, 2001

MacMichael, N.H., 'Filston in Shoreham: A note on the place-name.' AC LXX, page 133, 1962

McGreal, W. *Aylesford* (Friary). Canterbury Press, 1998

Page, E., 'Monastic Houses.' VCH II, 1926

Rosewell, R., *Medieval Wall Paintings*. Boydell, 2008

Wadmore, J.F., 'Tonbridge Castle and its Lords.' AC XVI, page 12, 1886

Zell, M. (ed), *Early Modern Kent, 1540-1640*. page 181-7, Boydell, 2000

Chapter 5: **THE REFORMATION TO THE RESTORATION** (pages 52-63)

Carly, J. and Hunter, J. (eds), *Valor Ecclesiasticus of 1535*. Record Commission, 1810

Chalklin, C.W., *Seventeenth- Century Kent*. Longman, 1965

Cockburn, J.S. (ed.), *Calendar of Assize Records, Kent, Elizabeth I*. HMSO, 1979

Cockburn, J.S. (ed.), *Calendar of Assize Records, Kent, Charles I*. HMSO, 1980

Everitt, A., *The Community of Kent and the Great Rebellion, 1640-1660*. Leicester University Press, 1966

Gee, H. and Hardy, W.J., *Documents Illustrative of English Church History*. Macmillan, 1896

Latham, R., *The Shorter Pepys*. Penguin, 1987

Melling, E. (ed), *Kentish Sources. II. Kent and the Civil War*. KCC, 1960

Rebholz, R.A. (ed.), *Sir Thomas Wyatt, the complete poems*. Penguin, 1978

Sorlien, R.P., *The Diary of John Manningham of the Middle Temple, 1602-1603*. The University Press of New England, 1976

Timpson, T., *Church History of Kent*. Ward, 1859

Twisden, J.R., *The Family of Twysden and Twisden*. Murray, 1939.

Chapter 6: **A LATE STUART AND GEORGIAN VILLAGE** (pages 64-93)

Andrews, C.B., *The Torrington Diaries between the years 1781 and 1794*. Eyre and Spottiswoode, 1954

Davidson, J., *Stream Cottage, The Stream, Ditton*. House Historians, (printed privately), 2005

Defoe, D., *Journal of the Plague Year*. Dent, 1962

Defoe, D., *A Tour through the Whole Island of Great Britain (1742-70)*. Penguin, 1986

Fuller, M. J., *The Watermills of the East Malling and Wateringbury Streams*. Christine Swift, 1980

Glynne, S., *Notes on Kent Churches*. Murray, 1877

Hague, W., *William Wilberforce*. Harper, 2007

Harrington, D., Pearson, S. and Rose, S., 'Kent Hearth Tax Assessment, Lady Day 1664.' page 163, The British Record Society and KAS, 2000

Harrison, E.R., *Harrison of Ightham*. Oxford, 1928

Hatton, R.G. and Hatton, C.H., 'Notes on the Family Of Twysden and Twisden.' AC. LVIII, page 43, 1945

Hills, R.L., *Papermaking in Britain 1488-1988*. Athlone Press, 1988

Marshall, W., *The Review and Abstracts of the County Reports to the Board of Agriculture*. Vol. V. Kent, page 413, 1817

Melling, E. (ed.), *Kentish Sources. I. Some Roads and Bridges*. KCC, 1959

Melling, E. (ed.), *Kentish Sources VI. Crime and Punishment*. KCC, 1969

Ogilby, J., *Britannia, Volume the first of the Kingdom of England*. Description of the principal Roads thereof. London, 1675

Severn, J., *The Teston Story*. Rufus Fay, 1975

Twisden, J.R., *The Family of Twysden and Twisden*, Murray, 1939

Warner, J., 'Dr John Warner's Visitations of the Diocese of Rochester, 1663.' Kent Records, new series, Vol. I, KAS, 1994

Wilson, M., *The English Chamber Organ*. Cassirer, 1968

Chapter 7: **A VICTORIAN VILLAGE** (pages 94-121)

Bagshaw, S., *History, Gazetteer and Directory of the County of Kent*. page 259, Sheffield, 1847

Hann, A., *The Medway Valley, a Kent Landscape Transformed*. Phillimore, 2009

Hobsbawm, E. J. and Rude, G., *Captain Swing*. Pimlico, 1969

Ingle, J., *Preston Hall – History and Legend*. Preston Hall, 1977

Matthews, M., *Captain Swing in Sussex and Kent*. The Hastings Press, 2006

Preston, J.M., *Industrial Medway: An Historical Survey*. J.M. Preston, 1977
Roake, M., 'Religious Worship in Kent. The census of 1851.' Kent Records 27, KAS, 1999
Sephton, J. H., *Preston Hall Aylesford*. James Sephton, 1997
Stratton, J.Y., *Hops and Hop-Pickers*. SPCK, 1883
Stratton, J.Y., 'The Life of a Farm Labourer.' *Cornhill Magazine*, Vol. IX, page 178, 1864
Stratton, J.Y., 'Farm Labourers, their Friendly Societies, and the Poor Law.' J. Roy. Agric. Soc.
England, Vol. 6, page 87, 1970
Tufnell, E. C., On the Dwellings and General Economy of the Labouring Classes in Kent and Sussex. page 36,
Sanitary Inquiry-England, 1847.
Vaughan, Mr, Reports of the Special Assistant Poor Law Commissioners on the Employment of
Women and Children in Agriculture. page 165, HMSO, 1843.
Yates, N., Hume, R. and Hastings, P., *Religion and Society in Kent, 1640-1914*. Boydell, 1994.

Chapter 8: **THE EARLY 20th CENTURY** (pages 122-154)

Brooks, R., *Kent Airfields Remembered*. Countryside Books, 1990
Clark, R. and P., *We go to Southern England*. Harrap, 1966. (A visit to Ditton Laboratory, pages 48-49)
Inglis, H.R.G., *The 'Contour' Road Book of England*. Gall and Inglis, 1923
Orwell, G., *A Clergyman's Daughter*. Penguin, 1964
Protheroe, R.E. (Lord Ernle)., *English Farming Past and Present*. Longman Green and Co., 1936
Warren, C.H., *A Boy in Kent*. Geofrey Bles, 1937

Chapter 9: **THE MODERN WORLD** (pages 155-169)

Carman, D., *Ditton Remembered: Past and Present*. 2003
Miller, E.P., *Ditton and Holt Wood; Conservation Studies*. Tonbridge and Malling Council, 1974
Sephton, J., *Preston Hall, Aylesford*. James Sephton, 1997
Syms, J.A., *Kent Country Churches*. Meresborough Books, 1984, 1987, 1989

Maps, manuscripts and other printed sources

Maps

A Book of Maps of the Estate of the Right Worshipful Sir Roger Twisden.
Surveyed and drawn by Abraham Walter and begun 1681.
(Includes maps of Borough Court and Ditton Farms)   CKS
A Plan of Ditton Court Farm together with six pieces of Woodland in the several Parishes of Ditton and
Aylesford, the property of the Viscountess Dowager Folkestone. Survey'd in the year 1772 by John Hart.
Bradbourne House, The East Malling Trust for Horticultural Research.
Borough Court Farm, circa 1775.   CKS

A map of West Kent surveyed by George Pink in 1789. British Library.
   (This is a very early Ordnance Survey map with a scale of six inches to the mile)
Map of Ditton Tithe Award, 1841. Copies in CKS and the Public Record Office, Kew.
Map of Preston Hall Estate of Edward Ladd Betts, 1849. Surveyesd by Frank Giles and drawn by T.J. West.
   (A very large map including much of Ditton)   CKS
Map of altered Tithe Rent charge for Ditton, 1892   CKS
Map of Ditton Court Farm. Undated late 19th century. Ditton Parish Council

Manuscripts

Ditton Parish Registers from 1663   CKS
Ditton Church, Churchwardens' Account Book from 1677   CKS
Ditton Overseer's Account Book from 1731   CKS
Ditton Parochial Schools. Log Books from 1863   CKS
Ditton Common Enclosure document, 1859   CKS
Ditton Parish Council, Minute books from 1894. Parish Council Office
The Court Baron of Brooke,   1788, 1848 and 1860   CKS

Printed Sources

Poll Books for the Western division of Kent 1837 and 1857   CKS
Particulars of sale of Ditton Place in 1905   CKS
Particulars of sale of Ditton Court in 1914   CKS

INDEX

Page numbers in heavy type refer to an illustration

Addington, 9, 11,13, 24, 33, 36, 52, 73, 155.
Agricultural labour, 98, 118.
Air Raid Protection (ARP), 143.
Allington, 9, 11, 15, 33, 52, 54, 122.
    Castle, 53, 54.
Allotments, 98-9, 133-4, 144.
Anglo Saxons, 30-32.
    Burials, 30.
    Chronicle, 30.
Ashford, 120.
Aylesford, 9-11, 14-5, 22, 25-26, 29-31, 34-35, 38, 41, 46, 59, 62,
    73, 75, 78, 80, 88, 94, 103, 105-6, 115, 118, 120, 122, 148, 161, 168
    Bridge **46,** 62, 75.
    Church (Minster), 31-2, 50, 93, 100.
    Earl of, 102.
    Friary, 40, 46, 53-4, 61-2, 87.
    Market, 47.
    Methodist Chapel, 102.
    Newsprint, 164, **165.**
    Paper Mills, 136.
    Royal Manor, 31.
    Station, 16, 105, 111.
    Swarling, 26.
Augustine, 30-1.

Banks family, 53.
Barham family, 47, 58.
Barham Court, Teston, 58, 66, 87.
Barming, 10, 14, 28, 32, 41, 60, 75, 118, 143.
Bartholomew, Frank (teacher), 118-9, **131,** 132.
Bayeux Tapestry, 33, 35, 37.
Bayham Abbey, 40.
Beaker People, 25.
Bearsted, 73.
Bede, 24, 30.
Bell Lane, 16-7, 22, 111, 116, 134, **135,** 136, 139, 148, 158,
    160-1, 168
Bellingham, Henry (farmer), 150.
Bennett, Henry (farmer), 142-3, **144,** 153.
Betts, Edward Ladd, 84, 99, 102-3, 105, 113.
Birling, 11, 13, 31-3, 52, 106, 155.
Black Death, 10, 38, 44-5, 58.
Blacklands, 108.
Blaze Wood, 35.
Blue Bell Hill, 29, 35.
Blue Cap Foods, 158.
Boghurst, William (apothecary), 65-6.
    Family, 65.
Bonnington, 41.
Bookland churches, 31.
Boreman, Jesper, (tanner), 66-8.
Borough Court, 10, 12-4, 16-7, 22, 47, 55-6, 66, 69, **70,** 97, 105,
    117, 133-4, 136, 148.
Boteler, Sir Oliver (Sen.), 58.
    Sir Oliver (Jun), 62-3.
    Sir Philip, 81.
    Sir William, 61-2,
    Family, 66.
Boundaries, 12.
    Stones, **12.**
Boxley Abbey, 39-40, 53.
Bradbourne House, 22, 29, 60, 68, 76, 81, **85,** 87, 141, 155
    Lane, 21, 56, 139-40, 143, 158, 165, 168.
Bramton, 38, 58.
    de Bramton family, 43.
Brassey, Henry A., 113,118.

Henry L.C., 122.
Thomas, 105, 113.
    Family, 122.
Brewer family, 56-7, 61, 66, 86, 163.
Brickworks, 115, 137.
British Legion Village, 155.
Broke Wood, 14, 16, 27, 83, 103, 166.
Bronze Age, 25-6.
Brooke Court (see Borough Court)
Bryant, Sir Arthur, 7.
Bunyan, John, 68.
Burham, 11, 22, 28, 33, 48, 84, 115, 118, 136.

Canterbury, 28, 30, 35, 38-9, 76.
    Archbishop, 33, 39.
    Diocese, 11, 31.
Capel, 46.
Carman, Don, 155, **157,** 162.
    Family, 134.
Cement manufacture, 115, 117, 136.
Charcoal pits, 15.
Charles I, 62.
Charles II, 63-4.
Charitable gifts, 59, 86.
Chart Hills, 10, 15, 23, 35.
Chatham, 148.
    Dockyard, 60.
Chaucer, Geoffrey, 39.
Church, St Peter's, 10, 13-4, 20-1, 31, 36-7, 41, **42, 44,** 45, 48, 50,
    52-55, 57, 64, **79,** 81, 86-7, **101,** 118, 124, **125,** 158, 161, 169.
    Attendance, 100.
    Bells, 63, 89, 121.
    Centre, 163.
    Church Rate, 87, 89.
    Gallery, 88.
    Memorials, 50, **56-7, 63, 86.**
    Music, 88-9.
    Organ, 86, **88,** 89, 100.
    Seating, 100.
Church Mill, 10, 13, 14, **23,** 66, 82, 87, 98, 134, **170.**
Churchscot, 31.
Churchwardens, 59, 78.
    Accounts, 87, 89, **90-1.**
Civil War, 61-3.
Clare, John (poet), 64.
Clare de, family, 41.
Clarkson, Thomas, 93.
Claudius, 28.
Cobdown, 13, 21-2, 30, 34, 72, 108, 155, 162, 165.
    Farm, 7, 10, 13, 17, 69-70, **71-2,** 79, 97, 107, **109,** 110, 117-8,
        127, 133-4, 148, **150,** 169.
    House, **108,** 133, 136.
Coldharbour, 15.
Coldrum Stones, 24.
Colepeper, Alice, 81 (Lady Taylor, Lady Milner).
    Elizabeth, 47.
    Sir Richard, 47.
    Sir Thomas, 81, 84.
    Walter, 47.
    Family, 54.
Community Hall, 162.
Conservation Area, 160-163.
Constables, Parish (Borsholder) 60, 79.
Coon,Thompson (farming family), 158.
Coppice woodland, **16,** 29, 60, 159, 166.
Cossington, 32, 41.

Countless Stones, 24.
Cromwell, Oliver, 62-3.
   Thomas, 54.
Cuxton, 9.

D-day, 28, 146.
Dartford, 72.
   Nunnery, 40.
Defoe, Daniel, 81.
Dictune, 9, 23, 168-9.
Dissolution of Monasteries, 51-52.
Ditton boundary, 12, 14, perambulation, 93.
Ditton Common, 7, 12, 14-5, 17, 22, 94, 99, 103, 133, 166.
Ditton Corner, 16, 62, 73, 108, 125, **130**, 136, 139-142, 144, 161.
Ditton Court (Farm), 10, 12-14, 17, 21, 47, 58, 61, 66, 81, **82**, 84, 86-7, 97-8, 107, 113, **114**, 122-3, **124**, 134, 138-9, 146, 150, 153, 157-8, 160-2, **168**, 169.
de Ditton family, 43, 45.
Ditton Green, 20, 34, 69, 78, 99, 106, 111, 113, 144, 150-1, 153, 160, 169.
Ditton Heritage Centre, 7, 163.
Ditton Laboratory, 138, 143-4, 146, **164.**
Ditton Manor, 12, 32-4, 36, 44, 47, 58, 61-2, 81, 84, 103, 113.
Ditton, origin of name, 9.
Ditton Park Estate, 140, 158.
Ditton Place, 10, 14, 34, 56-7, 66, 76, 86-8, 107, 109, **111**, 116, 121, 124, 134, 140, 142, 163.
Ditton Place Farm, 10, 13-4, 97, 125, 127, 142.
Ditton, Population, 9, 38, 94, 98, 113, 115, 118, 121, 143.
Ditton Street, 17, 111.
Dode, 41, **42.**
Domesday Book, 10, 22, 31-2, 34-6, 38-9, 168.
Dooner, Col. William, 124, 130, 159.
          Family, 129.
Dover, 28, 38, 62-3, 76.
Downderry Way, 141.
Drill Hall (Territorial Army) 162.
Duck, Stephen (poet), 98.

East Farleigh, 62.
East Malling, 10-11, 13, 14-15, 22-24, 27, 35-36, 38, 41, 43, 59, 66, 68, 77, 79, 94, 106, 113, 118-9, 122, 134, 154, 169.
   Church (St James) , 23, 28-9, 31-2, 45, 48, 54, 69.
   Fair, 95.
   Heath, 22, 62.
   Manor, 39, 47, 53, 73,
   Methodist Chapel, 102.
   Paper Mills, 108.
   Research Station, 123, **138**, 141, 145-6, 155, 164-6.
East Peckham, 38.
Eccles, 31, 33, 35, 115.
Education Acts, 107.
Edward the Confessor, 32-3.
   VIIth, 122.
Elections, Parish 126.
   Parliamentary, 97.
Electricity, generation, 139.
   supply, 139.
Elizabeth I, 55, 60.
Emigration, 118.
Ethelbert, 30.

Fairfax, Sir Thomas, 62.
Fernleigh House, 10, 128, **129**, 133-4, 159.
   Rise, 140, 156.
Feudal Aid, 45.
   Service, 43.
Field names, 17-19.
Fielding, Henry, 65.
Filmer, Sir Edward, 97.
Finch family, 53, 102.
Fitzhamo, William, 39, 43.
Folkestone, 127.
   Viscountess, 80, **81**, 82-3.
Football Club, 155, **156.**
Fox, George, 68.
Fruit growing, 29, 60, 138.

Garages, 142.
   SEECO, **142.**
Gas supply, 139.
Geary, Sir William, JP, 97.
Geology, 17-22.
Glebe land, 65.
Glynne, Stephen, 89.
Golding family, 78, 86, 163.
   John (Sen.) 86.
   John (Jun.) 88, 97, 109.
   Thomas (Sen.) 86.
   Thomas (Jun.) 59, 86.
   William, 77.
   Hop variety, 86.
Goodban, Harold, (teacher) **154.**
Goudhurst, 96.
Grey, de, family, 40.
Gundulph, Bishop, 36, 39.

Hadlow, 57.
Halling, 115.
   Church, 46.
Hamo, (Sheriff) 35.
Hart, John, (Surveyor), 80, 82-3.
Hasted, Edward, 9, 13, 73, 92.
Hatton, Sir Ronald, 138, **139.**
Hearth Tax, 66.
Hengist and Horsa, 30.
Henry I, 39.
Henry II, 36.
Henry VIII, 52, 54, 58.
Hermitage Farm, 41, 133.
Hodges, Thomas Law, M P, 85, 97, 120.
Holme, Rev. Edward, 106.
Holborough, 29, 30.
Home Guard, 143-4, 146.
Hop gardens and growing, 7, 60, 69, 86, 98, 109, 150, **153**, 158.
Hop picking and pickers, 78, 102, 104, 107, 151, **152**, 153.
Holt Hill and Wood, 15, 21-2, 24-25, 103, 134, 140, 142, 159, **160**, 163, 169.
Humphreys, Edward (Punter, cricketer) 117.
   Family, 117, 120.
Hunton, 9, 118.
Hythe, 73-4.

Ightham, 24.
Iron Age, 26-7, 29.
Iron production (Wealden), 29, 60.
Ivy House, 10, 127, 142.

Jole family, 65.
Julius Caesar, 28.
Jutes, 30.

Kent County Council, 120.
Kent Friendly Society, 102.
Kentish Petition, 61.
Kiln Barn, 13, 15, 20, 34, 66, 119-20, 125, 142, 146, 163, 169.
   Farm, 97, 134, 151.
   Road, 10, 64, 99, 113,**114**, 143, 160, 163.
Kinberley Clark, 155.
King(s) Hill, 73,
   Workhouse, 78, 96.
Kipling, Rudyard, 30.
Kits Coty, 24.
Knole House, 66.
Knoxes Shaw, 16.

Land Army, **145**, 146.
Laud, William, (Archbishop), 61.
Larkfield, 10-11, 14, 22, 29, 69, 102, 122, **128**, 133-4, 148, 158.
   Courthouse, 11.
   Cross, 41.
   Hall, 47, 117, 133, 155, 160.
   Hundred, 11, 44, 92.
          Turnpike Gate, 75.

Wealden Hall, 22, 47, 128.
Lay Subsidy, 43-4.
Lee, William, (Cement manufacturer), 117.
Lee Smith, Samuel, 117, 120, 133.
Leeds, 161.
　Castle, 39.
　Priory, 39-40, 44, 52, 55.
Leggatt family, 50.
Leigh family, 58.
Leybourne, 11, 32-3, 35-6, 54, 106, 142, 158.
　Grange, 54, 155.
　Wood, 35.
Lime kiln, 13, 66.
Linton, 9.
Local Defence Volunteers, see Home Guard.
Lollards, 51.
London, 36, 74, 76, 93, 95, 102, 105, 127, 161.
　Road, 16, 22, 73, 79, 111, 116, 124, 130, 139, 141, 144, 146, 148, 161.
Lone Barn, 10, 97, 134, 161.
Longsole Chapel (St Lawrence, Hermitage Lane), 32, 41.
Lovelace, Richard (poet), 61-2.
Luttrell Psalter, 43.

M 20, 73, 125, 161-2.
Maidstone, 10-11, 28-9, 38, 54, 62, 72-3, 78. 81. 89, 94-5, 105, 108, 118, 120, 146, 148, 150, 161.
Maidstone Assizes, 55, 57, 60-1.
Maidstone and District Bus Company, 141, 148.
Maidstone Grammar School, 93.
Maidstone Road, 16.
Maitland, Septimus, 111, 115.
Malling Poor Law Union, 11.
　Workhouse, 78, 96.
Malling Rural District, 11, 133, 139, 156, 169.
Manningham family, 60-1.
Maps, 5, 11, 14, 32, 74, 112.
　Borough Court, 70.
　Ditton Court Farm, 80, 82.
　Ditton Farm, 71.
　Field names, 18-9.
　Geology, 20.
　Monastic Houses, 40.
　Ogilby, 74.
　Symonson's, 5.
Mary, Queen, 54-5, 61.
Medway, River and valley. 9, 10, 12-3, 16, 22, 24-5, 28, 31, 34, 38, 46, 60, 69, 93, 105, 109, 113, 115, 118, 120, 125, 134, 142.
Mereworth, 35, 96.
Methodist Chapel, Aylesford, 102.
　East Malling, 102.
Mill Hall, 15, 34, 47, 60, 65, 161.
Mill Hall Mill, 7, 10, 13-5, 34, 66, 71-2, 87, 94, 98, 105, 134, 148-9, 162, 168.
Milner family, 81, 84, 103.
Mission Hall, Bell Lane, 118, 162.
Mortmain, Robert, **35.**
Motor traffic, 125, 130, 142.

Napoleonic Wars, 76, 78-9, 89, 96.
Nattes, John Claude (artist), 23, 78-9, 101, 170.
Nature Reserve (Quarry), 163.
Neath, Charlotte (teacher), 131.
Nettlestead, 35, 38, 93.
New Hythe, 10, 13-4, 47, 60, 109, 115, 134, 136, 155, 168.
　Chapel (St John the Baptist), 32, 41.
　Church, (Holy Trinity), 21, 102.
　Ferry, 118.
　Lane, 128, 161.
New Road, Ditton. 17, 22, 111, 125, 133, **135,** 140, 144, 147-8.
　East Malling, 17, 69, 85.
Normans, 31-8.
Norman Conquest, 31, 35-6.
North Downs, 24-5, 28, 35, 62, 73.

Oaken Wood, 14-5, **16,** 22, 54, 61-2, 66, 73, 83-4, 103, 166, 169.

Oast Houses, **104, 109,**111, 113, 124, 127, **150,** 151, 153, 158.
Odo (Bishop), 33, **35,** 37, 41.
Offham, 11, 33, 36, 38, 44, 52, 73, 75.
Ogg family, 159.
Ogilby, John (mapmaker), 73-4.
Old Ead Lane, 17, 168.
Old Mill House (Church Mill), 22, 48, **49,** 66, 122, 144.
Oldbury Hill, Ightham, 24, 27.
Orchard Grove, 7, 16, 140.
Orchard Place, 141, 148.
Oxford Movement, 95.
Overseer of Poor, 59, 76-9, 96.
Oxenhoath, West Peckham, 47, 97.

Paddlesworth, 11, 32, 41.
Palmars Rough, 15, 139.
Pannage, 35.
Papermaking and papermills.72-3, 94, 108, 134-6, **137,** 138, 141, 164, **165.**
Parish Council (Ditton), 120, 123, 125, **126,** 127, 130, 133, 139, 142-3, 146, 148, 162-3.
Park Farm, Bradbourne. 85, 133.
Penenden Heath, 33, 73, 161.
Pepys, Samuel, 63.
Peterhouse foods, 158, **159.**
Peto, Samuel, 103.
Piers Plowman, 45-6.
Pill Boxes, 144.
Plague, Great, 65-6.
Ploughing, **43, 123, 166.**
Pluralities Act of 1838, 95.
Police, County, 95, 97. (see also Constables)
Pope, Sir Thomas, 58.
Poor House, 78, 106.
Poor Law Amendment Act, 95-6, 102.
Poor Rate, 59, 77, 96 (see also Overseer of Poor).
Post Office, 148.
Preston Hall, 15, 21, 28, 47, 54, 81, **84,** 87, 103, **105,** 107, 113, 118, 120, 122, 129-30, 134, 139, 155, 161.
Pound (for stray animals), 99.
Priory Grove, 158.
Public House, 75, 87.
Pusey, Philip, 84, 97.

Quarries and quarrying, 20, 29, 78-9, 125, 142, 166.
Quarry Wood Camp, Loose, 27.

Railways, 95, 113, 119, 134, 168.
　HST, 163.
　London Chatham and Dover, 120.
　South Eastern, 105, 120.
　South Eastern and Chatham, 120.
Ramsay, James and family, 93.
Recreation Ground, 134, 136, 156.
Rectors of Ditton
　Archebolde, Nicolas, 54.
　Attke, George, 61.
　Bechynge, John, 51.
　Bishop, Samuel, 93.
　Burroughs, William, 100-1.
　Butler/Milner, Joseph, 84, 93.
　Hudson, Hugh, 50.
　Jackson, Theophilus, 64.
　Jole, William, 64-5.
　Kempe, Thomas, 52, 54.
　Prewe, William, 61.
　Scott, Philip, 7, 157.
　Skoye, Laurence, 50.
　Smith, Joseph, 65.
　Stammers, Frederick, 126, 131, 133.
　Stratton, John (see separate entry)
　Tilson, Thomas (sen) 65.
　Tilson, Thomas (jun) 93.
　Warde, Richard, 93, 97, 100.
Rectory, 10, 14, 61, 64-66, 82, **99,** 100, 115, 160.
Reed, Albert E., 134, **137.**
Reed's Paper Mills, 13, 134, 137, 139, 143, 148, 150, 155, 164-5.

175

Reform Act (1832), 95, 97.
Reformation, 51,
Richborough, 28.
River transport, 29, 47, 134.
Rochester, 28, 60, 76, 124.
Bishop, 33, 40.
Bridge, **38**.
Cathedral, 89.
Diocese, 11, 31.
Priory, 40, 44.
Romans, 28-9, 31.
Roman villas, 28-9.
Rome, 31, 52.
Rugmer Hill, Brenchley, 35.
Ryarsh, 11, 32-3, 36, 52, 62, 122.
Rycaut family, 53.
Sir Peter, 61-2.

Sandys, Col. Edwyn, 62.
School (Ditton), 21, 105-6, 118, **119**, **131**, 133. 144, **154**, 162-3.
Infants, 118, 162-3.
Library, 132.
Log Books, 107, 118, 127.
Scott, Sir George G. (architect), 101.
Sir Giles G. (architect), 130.
Thomas (farmer), 118, 122-3, 129, and family, 129.
Scottish farmers, 122.
Scouts, 123, 127.
Sedley family, 53.
Sevenoaks, 76, 120, 148.
Sewerage works, 139, 158, 162.
Shakerley family, 47, 55-6, 69.
Shakespeare, William, 58.
Sheldon Club House, 150, **151**.
Shoreham, 50.
Sifletone, Manor, 33-36, 41, 43, 58, 150.
Slave Trade, 93.
Snodland, 11, 28, 32, 115, 147.
Soulscot, 31.
Southampton, Earl of, 59.
Spicketts Wood, 15.
Spilman, John (papermaker), 72.
Springhead, East Malling, 23.
Stafford, Earl of, 41.
Statute of Labourers (1351), 45.
Stansted, 73.
Station Road, 16, 134, 136, 139, 147, 158.
Stocks, 72, 79.
Stone Age, 25.
Middle (Mesolithic) ,24.
New, (Neolithic), 24.
Stone Street, 28-9.
Stratton, Rev. John Y. 86, 101, **103**, 115, 118, **121**, 123, 125.
Publications, 102, **104,** 107.
Stream and ford, **3**, 9, 14, 22-3, 134, 147-8, 160.
Stream cottages, 10, 22, 48, 56, 66-68, 144, **145**, **157.**
Stream Lane, 94, **95**, 158.
Street lighting, 120-1, 139.
Strood, 105.
Style, Sir Robert, J.P., 76.
Swan family, 96.
Swing riots, 96.
Symonson's map of Kent, **5**, 15.

Tanneries, 22, 66-7, 87, 94, 170.
Tassell, Robert, 96, **108**, 109, 111, 118, and family 111, 118.
Teston, 15, 28, 54, 61, 75, 93.
Textus Roffensis, 31.
Thomas, John (architect), 103.
Tithe, 31, 36, 39, 65.
Tithe Commutation Act, 97.
Tithe survey, 15, 17, 97, 99.
Tonbridge, 76, 95.
Castle, 41.
Priory, 41.

Tonbridge and Malling Council, 163.
Tolhurst, Bernard (farmer), 129-30, 139.
Tomlin family, 69, 72.
Torrington, Lord, 75.
Tottington, 32-35.
Transportation, 79, 96.
Trottiscliffe, 11, 24, 36, 73, 155.
Turnpike Roads, 75-6, 119.
Twinning with Ditton, 163.
Twisden family, 43, 69, 85, 150.
Sir Thomas (First Baronet), **68**, 69.
Sir Roger (Second Baronet), 69.
Sir Roger (Third Baronet), 85.
Sir Roger (Sixth Baronet), 76-7, 81, 85.
Sir John (12th Baronet), **141**.
Twysden family, 61.
Sir Roger, 61.

Ulcombe, 63.
Uniformity, Act of, 64.

VAD Hospital, 127.
Valor Ecclesiasticus, 52.
Vermin payments, 89-90.
Vestry, 12, 58-9, 78, 120.
Victoria, Queen, 95, 118, 121, 127.
Vitalis, 33, 35, 37, 39, 43.
Vortigern, King, 30.

Wagon, Silas (Parish Clerk), 120.
Wall paintings, 46.
Walnut Tree, Public House, 75, 117, 140.
Walter, Abraham (map maker), 69-73.
Water supply, 138.
Wateringbury, 38, 96, 122.
Watling Street, 28, 38, 76.
Waywarden, 59-60, 78.
Well Wood, 12, 27-8, 166.
Wesley, John, 106.
West Farleigh, 36.
West Malling, 11, 13, 22, 35, 41, 47, 86, 94, 96, 104, 113, 118, 143, 147, 148.
Abbey, 36, 39, 40, 45, 52, **53**.
Airfield, 144.
Baptist Chapel, 102.
Church, 32, 36, 45, 48, 64, 89.
Magistrates Court, 97.
Market, 95.
St Leonard's Tower, 32, 36.
West Peckham, 36, 38, 96.
Wilberforce, William, 93.
William I, 31-33, 35, 39.
William II, 33.
Window Tax, 66.
Wiseman family, 58.
Woodlands Road, 140, 158-9.
Wordsworth, William, 169.
Working Mens Club, 123, 156, 162.
World War I, 127-131.
Memorial, **129, 130**.
World War II, 140, 143-7.
Bombing, 146.
Doodlebugs, 147,
Memorial, **147**.
Shelters, 143-4.
Wouldham, 11, 36, 115, 118, 136.
Wriothesley, Sir Thomas, 58.
Wrotham, 38, 54, 60, 73, 76, 118, 148.
Heath, 73, 75.
Wyatt, Sir Thomas (Sen), 53-4, **55**.
Wyatt, Sir Thomas (Jun), 54-5.
Wye College, 21, 122, 138.

Yalding, 93, 96.